P9-CKX-333

RICKS COLLEGE
DAVID O. McKAY LRC
REXBURG, IDAHO 83440

WITHDRAWN

DAVID O. McKAY LIBRARY
BYU-IDAHO

A Hole in the Wind

A Hole in the Wind

Hang Gliding and the Quest for Flight

Hank Harrison

The Bobbs-Merrill Company, Inc.
Indianapolis / New York

Copyright © 1979 by Hank Harrison

All rights reserved, including the right of reproduction
in whole or in part in any form
Published by The Bobbs-Merrill Company, Inc.
Indianapolis   New York

Designed by Robert Aulicino
Manufactured in the United States of America

First printing

Library of Congress Cataloging in Publication Data

Harrison, Hank.
  A hole in the wind.

  1. Hang gliding. I. Title.
GV764.H37   797.5′5   78-55645
ISBN 0-672-52400-7 hardcover
ISBN 0-672-52534-8 paperback

Acknowledgments

Foot-launched flight, hang gliding and wind surfing are all names used to describe the modern sport that, for the first time in history, has allowed human beings the freedom to fly on their own in relative safety. There are many professional books on the subject. Some are designed for advanced hang glider pilots and some for beginning pilots. Some of these books are accurate, some are controversial, some are thick epics, some are simple leaflets, and a few are extremely well written and well developed engineering manuals. Until now, there has been no technical book for the nonflier, no book for the family or the couple who may be curious about hang gliding but have small intention of attaching themselves to a wing and actually jumping from a cliff.

A Hole in the Wind is written for the people who want to sense the history and techniques of hang gliding without flying themselves. Some readers will go on to take a lesson, and some will be content simply to understand more about those curious bird-people occasionally seen on television or in the newspaper. It should be stressed that this is not a how-to-do-it book; it is rather a simplified explanation of some extremely technical information.

I owe a debt of extreme gratitude to George Harding and Francis Freeman, who often fly tandem at Sylmar, California; and to Rob Reed, the 1977 American National Champion, for their awareness of my project and for their encouragement in its planning. This is a book that fills a gap in hang gliding literature—a book for the curious.

I would also like to thank Bettina Gray of Rancho Santa Fe, California, and James Gillam, architect from Fairfax, California, for their direct contributions to the graphic quality of the book. The Dutch flying team Delta Team and the Bristol High School of Hang Gliding, Bristol, England, also deserve mention, since they helped me gain an international perspective on the sport. And I would like to dedicate this book to Nancy Jeffers-Cummings of the Clark County Library, Las Vegas, Nevada, for her total commitment to the book in its infancy.

Contents

Hang gliding the windmills, Wassenaar, Holland.

Harrison

1

The Flight of The Wind Dummy: Pre-Flight

For once you have tasted flight,
You will walk the earth with your eyes turned skyward;
For there you have been,
And there you long to return.

Leonardo
"On the Flight of Birds"

Hang gliding will be the ultimate sport of the twenty-first century because it reaches ahead in time and affords human beings of the late twentieth century an accurate view of future technology, especially the esoteric field of bio-engineering! The social systems surrounding hang gliding as a sport also give a glimpse of the kinds of political and psychological freedoms future generations may experience. In many ways, hang gliding is an accurate future index (as important as tool-making or bronze metallurgy to anthropologists), since it incorporates almost all aspects of modern life. In short, hang gliding is growing into an all-encompassing life style. It expresses the feeling and the reality of the last third of the twentieth century and combines the synergies of aerodynamics, space technology, metallurgy, soaring, sailing and gymnastics with electronics, photography, ecology and meteorology, but the newness of this life style does not diminish its effectiveness or longevity.

The enormous growth in hang gliding cannot be explained in simple terms. On cursory inspection, the sport seems to fulfill a public need for outdoor adventure that also establishes family and kinship ties between non-related groups of people. In some ways, hang gliding is a spontaneous attempt to establish new extended family identifications similar to sororities and fraternities in a world that has seen the unpleasant, but essential, breakdown of formal genetic families. Thus, hang gliding families, like rock-and-roll groups and surfers, tend to become tribal and territorial. The sport itself is rarely formal and never stuffy, even though the advanced pilots tend to feel a higher sense of spiritual consciousness than those who have only begun.

International hang gliding, competitive or otherwise, can also be seen as a loose-knit craft guild or trade union, with membership available to anyone with a modicum of athletic skill. Because of this availability, hang gliding has become both an art and a science, open to aesthetic expression and to technical experimentation, a kind of athletic alchemy which transcends language and cultural barriers. More important to the student of psychic history, hang gliding, in its evolving form, is a child of both ancient and modern research—research that has cost frustration, human lives and ridicule. Almost every pioneer of hang gliding, from pre-Christian times on, was ridiculed because, like it or not, he was upsetting the status quo.

For some reason not yet satisfactorily explained, individual foot-launched flight has always been a threat to the sedentary population. The idea of flight seems to symbolize rebellion and anarchy to the ultraconservative; actually this is not true. Someone who wants to fly on his or her own is simply pursuing an intuitive urge from deep within the subconscious, with no thought of politics. Still, the tracing of history shows that hang gliding has always been a kind of thorn in the side of the establishment, and free flights, especially successful free flights, have always been considered sorcery. Flying like the birds, let alone flying with the birds, seems to be an outlandish gesture; even the universal digit of discontent is referred to as "THE BIRD."

The lunar landings of the early 1970s accelerated and inspired the advancement of foot-launched flight, making it both commercially and emotionally feasible. The moon missions and reports from think tanks like the Club of Rome tended to soften public skepticism about the limits of human growth, and the old delineations of evolution had to be dumped. From that point on, hang gliding took on the guise of a continually recurring dream.

The dust of the violence and confusion of the 1960s settled around one precise and agreed-upon premise: Individual human freedom would be the goal for millions in the 1970s. There was no possibility of reversal; the chaff had been sorted from the wheat. In a crowded world, the right to become an individual became more important than temporal, political or secular values. Nothing was scoffed at any longer; anything and everything became possible. Few were ridiculed, even though their ideas were sick or passé, and the world view of the late 1970s became one of tolerance and vision. Only the faint and dying voices of older generations

Egyptian Sacred Stone showing human-bird figure ascending toward the sun, 1800 B.C.

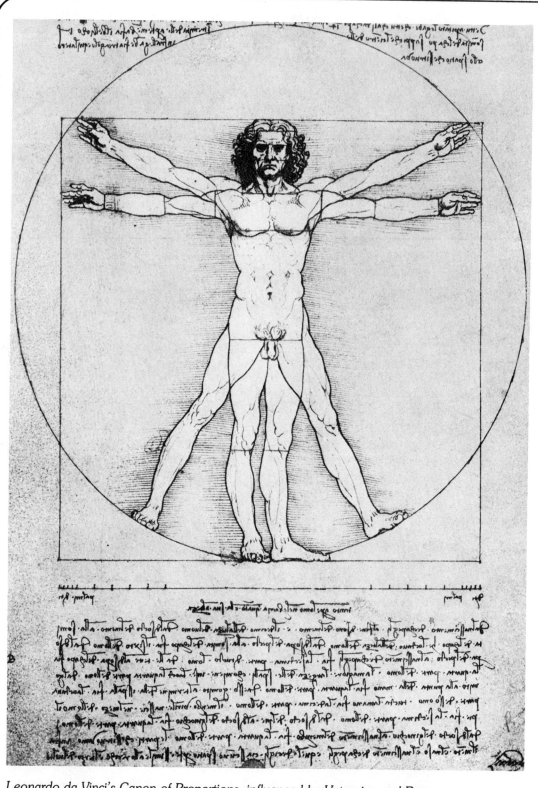

Leonardo da Vinci's Canon of Proportions, influenced by Vetruvius and Roger Bacon. This figure demonstrates that the arms of normal humans, when extended, are identical in length to the height of the body. Note mirror writing beneath the drawing.

whose dreams had already been actualized or else frustrated beyond repair could be heard in dissent. Goals of mass tribal conformity, both Marxist and capitalistic, no longer had survival value, except in a limited and immediate sense. From this nest the Phoenix of foot-launched flight emerged.

By the mid-1970s, hang gliding had become advanced and safe enough to allow a chance to fly to almost all who suffered from the need to dedicate their leisure time to the exploration of their own human potential.

Because of the upswing in the popularity of hang gliding, hang glider pilots were able to raise their public image from that of a bunch of simpletons out to explore new means of suicide to that of a new breed of pioneering futurists linked to Leonardo da Vinci. Without knowing it, they became radical activists, developing their physical bodies and their psyches simultaneously. By so doing, they inspired others to do the same, and a kind of logarithmic effect took over. Every time a press photographer took a picture of a hang glider pilot, a subtle chill went through the readers of that newspaper or magazine. At first, parents feared for the lives of their children, just as they had in the 1960s when so many ran away from home. But all was for naught—hang gliding was here to stay!

Even the toughest earth-bound neo-pagan motorcycle cultist (largely a product of the arch rebellion of the 1950s) stood in awe of hang glider pilots. Preliminary observation tends to support the conclusion that the bikers viewed the new bird-people and their cult as a society of braves and warriors like themselves. This attitude makes for further interesting speculation. Are hang glider pilots the soft-core rebels of the future? Is hang gliding replacing biking as a form of social dissent? Will the hang glider evolve into something as common as the motorcycle?

Spectators, watching modern sport gliders lift and fall, bank, cruise, dive and hover motionless on an invisible thermal, are still convinced that hang gliding is a fatally dangerous sport almost equivalent to a Kamikaze attack; nothing could be further from the truth! The aerodynamic technology that has made hang gliding a reality for thousands of men and women worldwide is extremely simple and safe, and the key to this safety is finesse.

Sports like swimming, track, basketball and football require major exertion. The major exertion required in short-flight, non-competitive, pleasure hang gliding is lugging the 20-kilogram wing up a hill or strapping it to the car at the end of the day. The aerodynamics of the glider do most of the work. Still, as with a sports car, there are limits to hang glider performance under various conditions, and there are hundreds of different glider designs. An ideal day for gliding is a day when the pilot has the most control, the most flight options; a dangerous day for hang gliding is a day when the pilot has only a small number of control options. Fools fly when saints repose.

Since competitive hang gliding was only rarely attempted prior to 1965, there is no accurate way to compare this new sport to any other activity. Surfing is hard work in an aquatic environment, and the surfer must often force the board to perform in balance with the waves. The Grand Prix driver must check on numerous variables: tire pressure, fuel conditions, speed, warning lights and other drivers, all the while taking real chances with life and limb. There are few moments of serene meditation. The scuba diver must be mindful of decompression times, and is dependent upon an artificial life-support system. In an even more complex way, a lunar astronaut, although seemingly isolated, is totally dependent on an incredibly long list of alien computer-based systems for survival and companionship.

The weekend hang glider pilot, on the other hand, is almost totally incommunicado once aloft. The life-support system is a dacron wing stretched across aluminum tubing, a helmet, and a parachute. Unlike other sports, which are performed in the simple four-dimensional aquatic environment, hang gliding provides the pilot an opportunity to touch the air. This experience provides a fifth-dimensional aerial view, sometimes referred to as a tune-in, and once the habit of tuning in is accomplished, it carries over into everyday life.

The benefits of any sport that combines danger with beauty and skill have long been noted by medical researchers. People who take risks and beat the odds are very healthy people; some may have death wishes, or rather the urge to cheat death, but most skilled danger-seekers are simply challenging life by pitting themselves against a difficult set of circumstances—the same kind of circumstances that caused Hillary to conquer Everest—"because it was there." This danger quest has heretofore been defined as psychopathy, but the truth remains that a crowded freeway on a rainy day is much more hazardous than hang gliding in hyperoxygenated clean air.

THE ANCIENT HISTORY OF HANG GLIDING

Both archaeological and mythical records bear testimony that human beings have long quested for flight. When this quest is considered objectively, some astonishing facts come to light. First and foremost, all of the

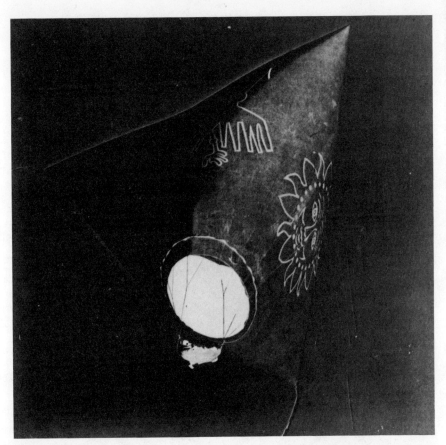

In 1973 a Canadian experimental team traveled to Peru and launched a hot-air balloon made from leather and linen. This balloon flew above the plains of Nazca, implying that the drawings on the desert could have been drawn by priests who had mastered the art of flight. This also reduces the flying saucer theory and indicates that ancient astronomers were extremely advanced.

ancient stories about fantastic birds, winged men, angels and magicians can be evaluated in a more literal context.

The parabolic glider is a very simple device, one that could have been invented by other generations in past societies. Although there is very little firm evidence that flight was achieved by many, there is some evidence that a few adventurous alchemists and priests did fly by various means.

It is unlikely that the cave dwellers who populated the earth at the end of the Ice Ages, such as Cro-Magnon, ever actually attempted to fly by constructing wings; but there is a great deal of information leading to the conclusion that these people did worship the sky and longed to join the birds. Many recent archaeological discoveries show that the cave dwellers managed to gain some kind of bird's eye view of their surroundings; they made maps and kept accurate records of weather and tidal conditions in order to monitor the sun and the moon and the animal migratory

Chartres labyrinth as a model of the solar system. A twelve-pointed star closes the maze, and a thirteen-pointed star opens it. The maze is identical in size to the rose window of the Cathedral, which is also a model of the solar system. Children's hopscotch games are also models of this maze, and anyone who walks the maze is said to be able to fly. This is a heliocentric model of the solar system, built 400 years before Copernicus.

patterns. In fact, the entire religion of the Ice Age peoples was based on stargazing and the tracking of the various moving planetary bodies.

In the formal religion of the Cro-Magnon world, total awareness of the universe was achieved by the tribal shaman during a trance. This awareness was, in turn, passed on to the tribe itself through stories. In other words, Cro-Magnon was able to achieve an *episcopic* (*epi*, above; and *scopi*, to see) view of the world. The shaman's experience was identical with what Buddhists now call Satori or what the Christian philosopher Teilhard de Chardin called Omega point.

Daedalus and Icarus

The labyrinth of life is represented by the myth of Daedalus and Icarus. Daedalus, the father, was imprisoned in a labyrinth with his son Icarus. After long suffering and aimless wandering in the maze, Daedalus was inspired to fashion wings from birds' feathers and candle wax. Eventually, the two managed to fly to freedom; but Icarus, the less wise of the two, soared too near the sun and quickly fell back to earth. The story of Daedalus and Icarus is considered an allegory showing that the haste of youthful folly can result in an abortive attempt to gain freedom. In other words, true freedom is gained slowly and with care. But could there not be a more literal meaning to this common old myth?

In 1971, an archaeologist named Charles Herberger, who also happened to be a poet and philosopher, discovered that the labyrinth of the Palace of Knossos in Crete was not the floor plan to the palace itself. True, the palace itself was a kind of labyrinth, but Herberger's further research proved that another special labyrinth was built away from the palace for a special purpose. This was an instructional labyrinth designed for solar research and observation of the sky.

These labyrinths were built and maintained for ritual purposes, connected with the Minoan government, which was a *theocracy*. The rituals conducted in the various mazes (and these labyrinths can be found throughout Europe, so evidently theocracy was widespread) had to do with observations of the stars and the sky, with flying, and with the worship of a winged bull-lion (Taurus-Leo).

The priests who maintained these transcendent places called themselves Daidalidai, and the labyrinths, which were also temples, were called Daidaleion. These little-known scientists were also artists, astronomers and engineers. They actually claimed to be descendants of the original Daedalus, or Daidalos, who flew out of the maze, the same Daedalus who constructed the labyrinth that confused Theseus and contained the Minotaur. The Daidalidai priests banded together to preserve ancient information and protect certain secrets. Was one of these secrets the key to the art of soaring with the birds?

There is little doubt that, possibly even before writing or agriculture was developed, ancient people from Asia, South America, Egypt and Europe had soared in their own kites or balloons or on tamed condorlike birds. Therefore, flying saucers are not necessary to explain the many vantage points throughout the world that need an aerial perspective to be understood.

The Great Snake of Ohio. This mysterious mound is, in itself, a model of the universe. In the winter the snake is eating; in the spring it is spitting out an egg, the universal symbol of life.

The Snake Mound in Ohio is only one example. The Giant Man of the Mojave is another, and still more exciting are the many markings on the desert in South America which show the clear outlines of hummingbirds, frogs and spiders. These drawings were first discovered in the early 1950s by Maria Reike, but their interpretations soon became perverted by flying-saucer enthusiasts who insisted that the markings were built by and for extraterrestrials. The truth is far more exciting. There is another strongly supported theory that all of these markings, even the beautiful Glastonbury Zodiac in England, were built by astronomer-priests and engineers like those in the guilds of Daedalus (and probably long before the time of Minoan Crete) who could, on occasion, fly or hover by various means. This is not to say they could will themselves upwards, as might be the case in the illusion of levitation, but that they had designed wings, balloons or kites of some sort. Further evidence is found in Chinese history. The ancient Chinese developed a man-lifter kite that was used in holiday ceremonies. Although flying was no secret to the Chinese, the technique was lost when the European public fell into many centuries of isolation during the Dark Ages. Europe in the Middle Ages had almost forgotten its own glorious pioneers, such as King Bladud and Simon the Magus.

From Bladud the Bard to the Flying Leonardo

Most hang gliding enthusiasts have heard of Daedalus, but almost no one has ever heard of the mysterious Bladud of Bath, known to the Greeks as Abaris the Hyperborean.

Bladud led many envoys to Minoan Crete and Athens. He was also the high priest and solar king of the early British tribes. The fact that King Bladud was a living historical figure is well documented; he was

Nazca Lizard. One of the many figures etched on the desert in Peru.

BLADUD,
To whom the GRECIANS gave the Name of
ABARIS.

King Abaris or Bladud was active in scientific investigations and was the first to introduce flying to Britain. After many flights, he fell upon the Temple of Apollo in London and was killed.

a Druid who reigned over Britain as its Tenth King between the years 863 and 843 B.C.

Although stricken with leprosy, Bladud was said to have in his possession a sacred bow and arrow and Sacred Wings that enabled him to fly. His son, King Lear, made famous by Shakespeare, carried on the tradition. The historian Geoffrey of Monmouth described Bladud as:

> A man of great ingenuity who taught magic [now known as science] throughout the land and abroad and finally making himself wings that enabled him to fly. [*Historia, Regnum Britannia*]

This stands as some proof that a king of England flew more than 800 years before Christ. Unfortunately, Bladud's reign came to an abrupt halt when he dashed himself to death in an accident over London. His Sacred Wings finally collapsed after 50 or more successful flights; but Bladud did, in fact, fly with wings of his own design.

During the time of Christ, roughly in the first century B.C., a magician and Gnostic named Simon Magus (not Simon the Apostle) was also able to fly, both by suspending himself from rods and cables and by fashioning wings of a sort. Unfortunately, he resorted to circus tricks to show the people his power as a messiah, but he did probably glide on homemade wings at more than one gathering.

After many successful flights performed in Phyrgia, Greece and Rome, accompanied by much fanfare, Simon Magus plunged to his death before a throng of thousands. This incident was portrayed, rather inaccurately, in a Hollywood film entitled *The Silver Chalice,* based on the 1952 book by Thomas B. Costain, in which Jack Palance played the role of the ill-fated Simon.

Octave Chanute, a completely sober American civil engineer and the teacher of the Wright brothers, filed these accounts of Bladud and Simon:

> Perhaps the earliest legend of an experiment which we may fairly suppose to have been tried with an aeroplane is stated to be found in the somewhat fabulous chronicles of Britain [Chanute refers to Geoffrey of Monmouth], wherein it is related that King *Bladud*, the father of King *Lear*, who is supposed to have reigned in Britain about the time of the founding of Rome, caused to be built an apparatus with which he sailed in the air above his chief city of London, but that losing his balance, he fell upon a temple and was killed. This is about all there is of the legend, and as even that concerning King *Lear*, which Shakespeare worked up into his

tragedy, has been suspected of being a myth, it is difficult to comment intelligently upon such a tradition; yet it is not impossible that King *Bladud* (who was reputed to be a wizard, as were all investigators in ancient times) should have attempted to imitate the ways of the eagle in the air, and should have succeeded in being raised by the wind, when, for lack of the balancing science of the bird, he should have lost his equilibrium, and with a shear, a plunge, or a whirl have come to disaster.

Chanute also elaborated on Simon Magus:

A better authenticated legend seems to be that of *Simon the Magician,* who, in the thirteenth year of the Emperor *Nero* (about 67 A.D.), undertook to rise toward heaven like a bird in the presence of everybody. The legend relates that "the people assembled to view so extraordinary a phenomenon and *Simon* rose into the air *through the assistance of the demons* in the presence of an enormous crowd. But that St. Peter having offered up a prayer, the action of the demons ceased, and the magician was crushed in the fall and perished instantly.

"It seems, therefore, certain" (adds M. *de Graffigny*) "from this tale, which has come down to us without any material alteration, that even in that barbarous age a man succeeded in rising into the air from the earth by some means which have unfortunately remained unknown."*

From the Dark Ages (between A.D. 300 and 1000), legends persist that Merlin the Magician, member of the court of Uther Pen Dragon and the teacher of King Arthur, was able to fly and to make things appear and disappear by use of a mysterious wand, sword or arrow, presumably inherited from Bladud and the other old Druids. It is not known if Merlin did in fact fly, but some legends portray him as having this ability.

Ancient flying stories would not be complete without mention of the fabled ninth-century Islamic hero Sinbad, who also possessed magical powers, including control of a Genji in a bottle. Sinbad managed to fly by taming a huge bird called a Rok, which transported Sinbad to all parts of the earth at the sailor's bidding. Obviously, this is an Arabic fantasy, but could it not have been derived from some more literal and realistic truth

---

* From O. Chanute, *Progress in the Flying Machine*, New York Engineering Society, 1894.

passed down through generations by oral tradition? In modern times, on the pampas of Argentina, gauchos ride ostriches for sport, so it is not a great stretch of the mind's eye to imagine ancient peoples taming condors or other birds that would afford them an occasional pioneering flight.

Then there is a legend of the eleventh century concerning Oliver of Malmesbury, who in some of the accounts is called Elmerus de Malemaria. Oliver, an English Benedictine monk, was said to have been a student of mathematics and astrology, thereby earning himself a reputation as a wizard. The legend relates that:

> . . . having manufactured some wings, modeled after the description that *Ovid* has given of those of *Dedalus*, and having fastened them to his hands, he sprang from the top of the tower of Malmesbury Abbey in Wiltshire against the wind. He succeeded in sailing a distance of 125 paces; but either through the impetuosity

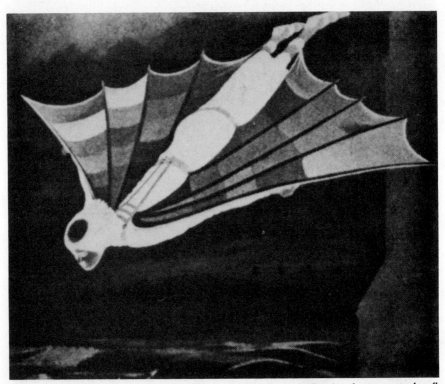

Oliver of Malmesbury, a monk of Malmesbury Abbey in England, attempted to fly from the arches of the Abbey. He was crippled for his efforts and blamed Halley's Comet for his failure. He realized that he should have affixed some sort of rudder to his contraption, but it was too late. Oliver died a hermit while still a young man.

or whirling of the wind, or through nervousness resulting from his audacious enterprise, he fell to the earth and broke his legs. Henceforth he led a miserable, languishing existence (he died in 1061), attributing his misfortune to his having failed to attach a tail to his feet. [Bescherelle, *Historie des Ballons,* 1852]

Commentators have generally made sick jokes over this last remark, but, in point of fact, it was probably pretty near the truth. To perform the maneuver, Oliver of Malmesbury must have employed an apparatus somewhat like a gliding bird, but to balance himself fore and aft, as does the bird by slight movements of its wings, head and legs, he would have needed a larger tail.

A more specific example of early hang gliding comes from Constantinople. About 1178, during the reign of the Emperor Manuel Comnenus, an unnamed Saracen (reputed to be a magician, of course) undertook, in the presence of the Emperor, to sail into the air from the top of the tower of the Hippodrome. The quaint description of this attempt, as taken from the history of Constantinople by Cousin and quoted both by Graffigny and by Bescherelle, clearly describes a hang glider and indicates very well the difficulty of maintaining a proper balance.

He stood upright, clothed in a white robe, very long and very wide, whose folds, stiffened by willow wands [battens], were to serve as sails to receive the wind. All the spectators kept their eyes intently fixed upon him, and many cried, "Fly, fly, O Saracen! do not keep us so long in suspense while thou art weighing the wind!" [I.e., adjusting the angle of incidence and the equilibrium of the machine.]

The Emperor, who was present, then attempted to dissuade him from this vain and dangerous enterprise. The Sultan of Turkey in Asia, who was then on a visit to Constantinople, and who was also present at this experiment, halted between dread and hope, wishing on the one hand for the Saracen's success, and apprehending on the other that he should shamefully perish. The Saracen *kept extending his arms to catch the wind.* At last, when he deemed it favorable, *he rose into the air like a bird;* but his flight was as unfortunate as that of *Icarus,* for the weight of his body having more power to draw him downward than his artificial wings had to sustain him, he fell and broke his bones, and such was his misfortune that instead of sympathy there was only merriment over his misadventure. [Cousin, *History of Constantinople*]

This account seems to be authentic, and the apparatus was obviously some form of hang glider or parachute, because it is likened to a robe and a pair of wings, and also because no mention whatever is made of any flapping action. The only exertion on the part of the Saracen is adjusting the handmade wings to the prevailing wind. This action implies that the angle of incidence could be regulated to achieve soaring.

Only brief allusion need be made to the writings of Roger Bacon, a Franciscan mystic philosopher of the thirteenth century (1214–94). He prophesied the invention of both the balloon and the flying machine, but did not actually try any experiments himself. His importance comes from his flying visions, found in the Franciscan encyclopedias, which greatly influenced Leonardo da Vinci. Both men were obviously initiated into a secret society of magicians, probably an early version of the Society of the Rose Cross, also known as the Priory of Zion.

Of course, there were a few experiments before da Vinci's. In one such experiment, a philosopher named John Dante (not the author of the *Inferno*) successfully flew a hang glider over Perugia, Italy, in the fifteenth century. It is not known whether Dante grew overbold with early successes, or whether he was forced to display his achievement before his fellow-citizens and his king prior to a thorough pre-flight test. In any case, he attempted to repeat his flights on the occasion of the marriage of a prince named Bartholomew Alviano. Starting from the top of the highest tower in the city, Dante sailed across the public square and balanced himself for a long time in the air, amid the applause of the festive crowd. Unfortunately, the iron forging which managed his left wing suddenly snapped, and he fell upon the Cathedral Notre Dame and broke his leg. Upon recovery, he seems to have given up further experiments. He went to teach mathematics at Venice, where he died of a fever before he had reached forty. If this story is true, Dante's hang glider must have been more manageable than any of its predecessors, for the accident is said to have been due to a breakage instead of a loss of balance. It is unfortunate that no detailed description of the machine and its mode of operation has survived.

Two somewhat similar experiments are alluded to in M. G. de la Landelle's "Aviation," published in 1863, but the descriptions are too brief to give much of an idea as to the kind of hang glider employed. *Paul Guidotti*, an artist-painter, sculptor and architect who was born in Lucca in 1569, constructed wings of whalebone covered with feathers, and made use of them several times with success. Determining to exhibit his discovery, he took flight from an elevation, and sustained himself in the air for a quarter of a mile; but he soon became exhausted, and, like Dante, fell upon a roof, breaking his thighbone.

Near the same time, Francisco Orujo, a Spaniard, was said to have sailed in the air approximately 20 minutes with artificial wings. He covered a distance of about three-quarters of a mile, or one kilometer.

In spite of these other earlier tales of valor, it was Leonardo da Vinci who made the highly technical breakthroughs that allowed modern windsailing to develop. Through his esoteric studies, Leonardo reached the conclusion that Icarus, Bladud, Simon Magus and untold others had plunged to their deaths or seriously injured themselves by attempting flight with inadequate knowledge. The urge to soar was so strong that they gambled their lives against the hope of joining the gulls and falcons. Perhaps if they had taken fewer chances, they would have survived. But the quest for flight was infinitely more exciting than the life of a monk or a merchant. In any case, Leonardo had no illusions. He applied systematic experimentation that canceled most of the risks. With Leonardo, flight became a science; yet it must be stressed that Leonardo toiled in secret, disguising his research as an effort to develop spectacles and stage illusions for his patrons. The political atmosphere of the time was dogmatic and repressive, and many powerful people were horrified by untried ideas.

Other Strange Pioneers

A close look at the history of human flight reveals that aeronautical science managed to advance when certain individuals openly yearned for the freedom of the sky, or in some way made their discoveries available to at least a few other experimenters. The greatest advances were made when actual flights were made before many witnesses.

In the one thousand years between 500 B.C. and A.D. 500, a great many thinkers asserted that human beings were capable of wing-aided and foot-launched flight. After the sixth century, however, actual experiments and outspoken dreams of flight were considered heretical and were punishable by death. In spite of those prohibitions, the archetypical dream of flying persisted quietly, almost as if foot-launched flight were part of human destiny.

Even in the so-called Renaissance, the age of Leonardo da Vinci, all thoughts of mathematics and technological breakthroughs in science were held back by superstitious propaganda circulated by moral wardens everywhere. In 1600 Giordano Bruno was burned at the stake for publishing the mathematics and science of Copernicus and his own rather odd ideas on memory and magic. In this environment the average human

An angel appears to an alchemist. Note the profusion of symbols around the room, especially the Phoenix rising from the Holy Grail on the table, and the alchemist's oven in the left foreground.

being was led to believe that flight was equal to demonology and that thoughts of flight were mere hallucinations of levitation. The Inquisition interpreted the wish to fly as a betrayal of the person's secret wish to stray from the flock. The closed mind, wherever it occurred in history, always thought of flight as the province of witches who changed into crows, necromancers who cursed crops, or bats that sucked the blood of babies. The only wings that were permissible were the wings of angels like Michael

John Dee and Edward Kelley, two Elizabethan magicians, attempt to bring up a spirit in the churchyard. This type of activity was frowned upon by the Church authorities but was privately franchised by the Crown.

or Gabriel or Ariel, who swooped down to earth both to save and to pass judgments on those who prayed dutifully.

The study of various church documents, especially the records of the Renaissance heresy trials, proves time and time again that the urge to be free was symbolized by human flight, and the natural desire to be free has never been fully erased from public consciousness. It is almost as if humans were chosen to fly and nothing, not even torture or the fear of death, could stop this desire.

Later documents from the sixteenth and seventeenth centuries clearly establish that various witches were thought to fly through the air on brooms and to possess certain ointments and balms which, when rubbed on the skin, enabled the user to fly. This alone was enough to cause normal Christians—even to the present era—to equate flying with paganism.

The hysteria over human flight is best exemplified by two mystics within the Church itself. Both Saint Theresa of Avila, a Carmelite, and Padre Cupertino, a Franciscan, were said to possess the ability to fly at will; and their flights seem to have been witnessed by unimpeachable authorities. (Of course, yoga masters and tantric Buddhist gurus in Tibet have long claimed that levitation was a reality; but in Asia, this is not considered an abnormality.)

In Spain, in the 1560s, while Leonardo was at the height of his research, Saint Theresa was said to be levitating, empowered by the spirit of God. She was often seen floating both in a golden aura in her chambers and above the ground in her garden. She was investigated by numerous councils prior to canonization.

The other incident occurred approximately one hundred years after the death of Saint Theresa. Padre Cupertino, or Coppertino, flew in his courtyard, motivated by the will of God alone. To assuage the worries of his immediate curate, he was taken before the Pope himself for investigation. The Padre knelt in devout prayer for some thirty minutes and then, to the amazement of all, willed himself into the arms of a statue of the Virgin which stood some fifty feet across the room. Unfortunately, Padre Cupertino had some sort of nervous breakdown after achieving this feat and remained in cloister for the rest of his life.

The Christians were alone in reporting flight dreams as heretical or hallucinatory. The Chinese and Arabic world was convinced that real flight was a religious experience of great import. In Bengal, India, prior to the year 888, a Mogul named Abdul Kuasim Abbas bin Firnas built and flew a hang glider. It is assumed that this kind of activity was not frowned

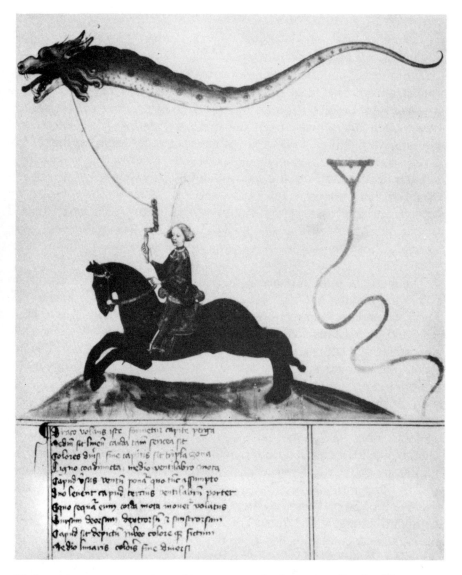

Medieval horseman carrying a kite as a standard representing the Dragon, an esoteric symbol of transcendence. These kites were used in combat to aid archers and to frighten the enemy.

upon, since he flew many times, injuring himself only on the first flight. Eventually, Abdul became a novelty at court and entertained many spectators with his custom-made wings constructed from thin silk and reeds.

There is, however, no point in discussing hang gliding as a purely historical phenomenon, since the history must be viewed through the eyes of a modern hang glider pilot or spectator. It is important to provide contrasts—flashbacks and flashforwards—because hang gliding evolved in that fashion. Great advances were followed by massive setbacks. Da Vinci discovered this phenomenon and experienced it himself, as did Sir George Cayley. Perhaps a flashforward to a first lesson in hang gliding will be of assistance.

Flying north, Torrey Pines, California.

Bettina Gray

2

Cripple but Free: True Flight

*From the mountain that takes its name from the
big bird, the famous bird will take its flight,
which will fill the world with his great fame.*

Leonardo
"On the Flight of Birds"
Folio 18, verso
Paragraph 2, recto

Watching modern hang glider pilots soar at Kossen, Austria, in the Alps, at Grandfather Mountain in North Carolina, at Mount Fuji in Japan, at Torrey Pines near San Diego, or off the cliffs in Wassenaar, Holland, can be an experience almost as uplifting as flying. However, as in most sports, a gathering of fools can cause a gathering of dolts. When hang glider pilots play to the crowd and take chances, hang gliding deteriorates into a blood sport. The mob mentality frequently demands violence. Although hang gliding is greatly removed from combat, any crowd can demand blood if it is so encouraged by media managers and big-time sports conglomerates. Luckily, the professional hang gliding community is tight-knit, and the professional pilots are well organized. They themselves demand a great deal from the sport and from the governing associations because they realize, more than anyone else, that the real thrill in foot-launched flight is in the appreciation of life and the balance of the universe.

The responsibility for conditioning spectators, especially those who will never fly, rests on the shoulders of the pilots themselves, since hysterical rumors, often exaggerated on re-telling, seem to have originated with pilots. Braggadocio is not necessary in hang gliding. Because only learning, thorough study and extensive training can clarify the sport, prior to the 1970s very few people except advanced pilots had any real appreciation for the aerial ballet, the sky dance that is intrinsic in windsailing.

Crash dives, although spectacular, are very rare in hang gliding, and few end in fatalities. It is natural for people who will never fly to observe hang glider pilots and their maneuvers in awe, but no one should ever expect a crash.

Statistics kept by the United States Hang Gliding Association and by other international organizations show that hang gliding accidents are rare in proportion to the number of hours flown and the number of flights launched per pilot. In 1975, when popular hang gliding was in its infancy, rated pilots in all classes logged more than 200,000 official flights, yet there were only 1,100 accidents reported. Out of these, only 12 resulted in fatalities, fewer than the number of fatalities reported in snow skiing. Now, due to even more rigorous control by the governing bodies, this ratio has been diminished, and hang gliding deaths and accidents are rare compared to the thousands of flights launched. This happy circumstance is due to the hang rating system and a number of other safety precautions. The hang rating system, as developed by the United States Hang Gliding Association (U.S.H.G.A.), is mastered in stages of competence, such as Hang I, Hang II, etc. The European system is almost identical except that the stages are called Pilot I, Pilot II, etc.

Safety improvements have come from both the pilots and the manufacturers. Active hang glider pilots, especially professionals, perform rigorous pre-flight checkups before every flight and every breakdown and re-setup of the hang glider. Another factor in improving accident ratios stems from the extensive and rigorous flight training required for certification. There have also been vast improvements in harness design, sail structure, wing tension integrity, aluminum tube quality, electronics, safety equipment and flight techniques. The physical conditioning and the psychological set of the pilot are also factors.

Hang glider pilots now think of themselves as conditioned athletes who are ready for anything. Most of the championship pilots studied are involved in yoga or some other form of meditation coupled with calisthenics, jogging, bicycling or some other physical exercise program; they also practice good nutrition. For example, one woman champion is also a modern dancer. She wears a full leotard under her flight suit and flies in ballet slippers to lighten her overall load. To her, flying is an extension of the dance. She has never had an accident and never takes dares.

FIRST THINGS FIRST: THE HANG I RATING

Most training schools teach the student that the glider itself is tougher than it looks. It is no sin to bang a training glider into the dirt on the first few flights. In fact, one's first flights, like Lilienthal's, da Vinci's and others', must be ground skimmers, flights that take place no more than

Poor landing technique.

Bettina Gray

Hang I pilot rating will require a straight-line solo flight and a number of hours of training.

three meters above the ground and function along a straight-line trajectory. By definition, ground skimmers last only a few seconds and traverse less than 30 meters; but these flights provide the first tastes of soaring.

Obviously, many first flights are going to end with scraped knees or elbows, but pilots can avoid unnecessary mishaps by logging a few hours in a static trainer. This device employs a harness in which the pilot can experience almost all of the usual body movements prior to actual outdoor flight. Naturally, the glider itself in the open air is a bit more slippery and certainly more responsive than a static trainer; but a static trainer can provide a great deal of muscle memory, and this increases safety.

Ground School

In the early 1970s, spectators stood on the ground and followed the flights of the newfangled kites with varying emotions. Even now, asked for their opinions, any two spectators will contradict each other. One will say, "Damn fools! They're crazy!" The other will say, "Boy, that looks easy!" Both of these statements are extreme. Anyone who has attended even one flight school for hang gliding can testify that hang gliding is neither crazy nor easy. It's like any other sport. For example, a pro makes golf look easy, but anyone who gets out there on Saturday with the other hackers and tries to get that little white ball in the cup in three or four strokes knows it isn't easy! The same illusion of simplicity holds true for chess, surfing, sailboating and many other activities. The illusion of ease is achieved only through long practice.

The most difficult first step in hang gliding is learning to relax in the harness, but it must be achieved. A change of direction or lift is achieved by a simple push on the control bar or a simple shifting of the point of central gravity. In some cases, a shift of 3 inches can mean a lift of 13 feet, so a tense, panicky push or pull of 2 feet can mean disaster. Because the moves of hang gliding are so unlike those of other sports, ground-school training is essential.

Ground-school lesson costs are nominal. Approximately $200 puts the trainee into a borrowed hang glider and prepares him for some gradual-slope flight and a few short first glides. The hang gliders, for the most part, are constructed of aluminum tubing covered with heavy-duty dacron sail material, the same material used on racing sailboats. The straps and harnesses are made of nylon and steel and are of aircraft-grade construction. The tensioners and connectors are constructed of high-test steel.

Selecting the wing. In the early days of the sport, the majority of wings put into the air as hang gliders were Rogallo gliders, named after Francis Rogallo, who developed the shape and basic mathematics of the delta-winged glider. Most ground schools still use Rogallo kites as basic trainers.

The basic Rogallo wing achieves buoyancy when the ground speed reaches 25 kilometers per hour, or when the combined head wind and ground speed equals 25 kph. The design of the kite is of great importance. Although some wings lift off at greater or lesser speeds, 25 kph is an industry average. The average weight of a hang glider is less than 25 kilograms, or 55 pounds.

Flight Positions

Seated position. The seated position is traditional for hang gliding. The pilot takes off by running, and when the wing achieves buoyancy, the pilot leans back into the harness and sits across a padded nylon strip that is part of the harness. The seat is loosely strapped to the upper part of the legs so that it cannot slip off at the critical moment of lift-off, but it and the harness must be adjusted properly before the pilot starts running. As soon as lift-off occurs, the glider pilot must gain control of the wing. A few seconds spent in adjusting the seat or harness could spoil the takeoff and cause control loss.

Prone position. The prone position is growing in popularity; it is the best position for viewing the ground below and is not dangerous. In fact,

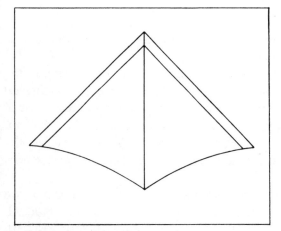

Standard Rogallo Wing Shape

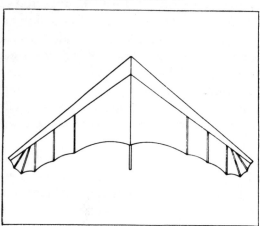

Radical Batten Tip Wing Shape

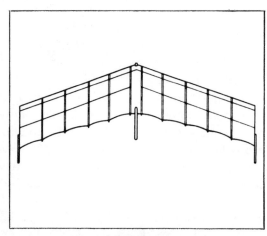

Fixed Wing Shape

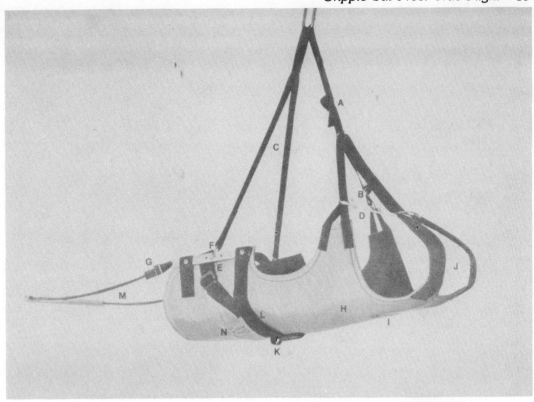

A TORSO HEIGHT ADJUSTMENT
B CHEST TENSION ADJUSTMENT
C 4000 LB. TEST SUPPORT WEBBING
D SHOCK CORD ANTI-DROOP SUPPORT
E ALUMINUM SUPPORT BAR
F PILOT   ADJUSTMENT
G ADJUSTABLE STIRRUP LINES

H 1/2" ENSOLITE FOAM PADDING
I ONE GENUINE SEAGULL AIRCRAFT PATCH
J ENSOLITE FOAM SHOULDER RESTRAINTS
K VELCRO STIRRUP HOLDER
L RAP-AROUND SAFETY WEBB
M CLEAR PLASTIC TUBE STIRRUP LINE STIFFENERS
N RUNNING "W" STITCHING

SOARING PRONE HARNESS

SUPINE SEAT HARNESS

Examples of prone and seated harnesses.

flying prone is safer for takeoffs, because in this position, the pilot leans forward over the controls, while the lift of the wing pulls the harness into the control position almost automatically.

Combined position. In 1975, a combination harness was introduced that allows the pilot to choose either of the above positions. This harness is advantageous to those who wish to soar for long periods of time, as one can shift positions to relax. The seated position is better for waiting out a lot of dead air, also called green air, while the prone position is probably better for dealing with erratic conditions.

The classic Rogallo launch technique is to bend down and lift the glider by wrapping the arms around the upright control frame and lifting the glider with the control bar. Most bars are roughened or taped to mark grip points, but this is an individual adjustment. The control frame is triangular, so standing in the center of the frame and lifting the hang glider causes the shoulders to contact a narrow portion of the triangle, the exact location of which is dependent upon the pilot's height and girth. Many pilots customize their gliders by wrapping foam padding around these contact points, since it is often necessary to hold the weight of the glider for long periods of time while waiting for wind conditions to improve prior to takeoff. In this way, the shoulders do the lifting, and the arms and grips merely control the static sway.

Flight instructors never allow beginners to practice in winds that may cause a blowover, since clumsiness and seeming failure at this point can be discouraging. Hot rods who wish to advance too rapidly rarely care if the glider tips over; but less adventurous people become discouraged easily. If hang gliding is to become a genteel sport, it must be taught in a genteel manner, one step at a time. Wind that is only a pleasant blow to the Sunday walker can be an incredibly fickle enigma to inexperienced trainees with 70 meters of sail hitched to their backs.

The pilot must learn to be natural in lifting the glider and carrying it up a small hill. This is clumsy, awkward and exasperating at first, but essential. Like an aqualung, a glider, once buoyant, is a dream machine, but on the ground with no wind, it tends to be cumbersome. Beginning pilots soon learn that the glider must be thought of as a working tool that acts properly only when airborne.

The Walk-around Technique

A walk-around inside a building or a large hangar can show the neophyte a great deal about the handling characteristics of a hang glider. This exercise entails walking approximately one kilometer each day with

Harrison

Fort Funstan, San Francisco.
Running into ridge lift, hands in ground control position.
First "Pop." Note hand position.
Once aloft, hang glider does most of the work.

the glider fully extended above. The walk-around also tells the beginner a little about future aches and pains and the need for conditioning.

Once outside, with practice and a slight wind, the pilot can make the kite lift most of its own weight by putting the nose of the kite into the wind and walking up the hillside; but he or she still needs fine muscle control to moderate sideward drift, because it is easy to fall or twist an ankle.

Hang I: Step II—Control Phase Shift

To get from the standing position to the prone flying position, the hang glider pilot must move his or her arms from the lifting position to the control position. This is best learned in a static trainer, but it will also have to be learned in the actual first-flight situation. To take off, the pilot must quickly unwrap the arms from the lifting position and replace this grip with an arms-forward grip. This repositioning technique seems simple, but it is critical and must be learned perfectly. Learning to shift to the control position prior to flight will give the pilot confidence. This movement can prove to be very frightening and confusing under actual first-flight conditions, because the beginning flyer's body first becomes dependent on a hanging harness during this maneuver. When the hang glider becomes buoyant, the pilot must immediately undergo three unfamiliar sensations. First, the shift in control position must be made smoothly and directly. Second, when the body weight becomes dependent on the harness for the first time, the pilot experiences sway, down-sink, and forward motion. Third, the pilot's feet must hook into the guide stirrup. No pilot can be in control of the glider until these three unearthly feelings become second nature.

Hang I: Step III—First Lift

A basic Rogallo glider takes off when its forward motion reaches approximately 21 kph. This means, for example, that when the wind is approaching the kite at 15 kph, the pilot must run into the wind at a speed of 6 kph to achieve full buoyancy. The trainee should make many practice runs up to the point of buoyancy but no further. This familiarizes the pilot with actual outdoor conditions without unnecessary knee landings. This run-and-stop technique must be practiced until the grip switch and the lift experience have been mastered. Training in this technique also lessens the psychological shock of the first long soaring experience and thus enhances the emotional pleasure of first flight. If these steps are followed under the guidance of a competent instructor, they soon become automatic.

First cliff soar comes after many hours of preparation.

Hang I: Step IV—First Cliff Soar

Wind is the master of the air. Top instructors always warn new pilots away from crosswind on the first flights. Even professionals rarely try crosswinds, just as top surfers never take a choppy wave if it can be avoided. As a wind surfer, the pilot must be cognizant of wind; all first flights must wait for ideal conditions.

When wind conditions are ideal, the instructor will sanction the first flight. To fly, the pilot will repeat Steps I through III, but this time he or she will not balk; he or she will fly a short distance down the hill or off the practice cliff, to a stand-up landing. For the first few flights, the pilot should not rise more than 2 meters above the ground. On these flights the instructor usually controls the kite's nose with a lanyard or tether which can pull the nose down if it begins to flare too high. These first flights must be guided to avoid later discouragement.

At this early stage, a jerky push forward will invariably end in a fall, a sharp tuck will probably lead to a sharp dive, and a rough push can translate into an unwanted lift. On first flights, all the pilot needs is a straight line down the hill and a safe stand-up landing. If the pilot can do this properly and unhook the carabiners from the riser strap immediately upon touchdown, most instructors will award the pilot the Hang I rating. The pilot will probably feel as Orville and Wilbur Wright, King Bladud of

Bath, and Leonardo felt when they flew for the first time—a bit frightened, but elated and triumphant.

By successfully flying a hang glider down a simple hill, the pilot has duplicated the past miracles of Simon the Druid and Sinbad the Sailor and has caught a glimpse of the future.

Instructor holds student prior to launch.

Hang I: Step V—Landing

All pilots must land eventually. Landing is not the kind of thing that can be learned as the instructor shouts at the pilot from the ground through a megaphone or bullhorn, although some schools do use radios. Landing is the final pirouette in the aerial ballet; and although the pilot has not flown more than 10 meters above ground, all flight ends in landing, just as if the pilot had descended from an altitude of 4,000 feet. Furthermore, this landing technique must be performed correctly the first time.

Landing a hang glider is defined as an aerial stall at leg distance from the ground. At high altitudes, stall is a mixed blessing—it can be a very dangerous maneuver or a fine way to slow down a dive. But stall is essential for landing. Some experts call the technique flare, and some call it bleed-out or bleed-off. In basic Rogallo flying, as in the flight of birds, forward motion creates natural air circulation under the wing, which in turn creates lift. In mid-flight, this under-wing air rotates smoothly, but when the hang glider pilot approaches the ground, the rotation becomes turbulent, the lift is almost doubled, and the flight can

Sighting the spot.   Shooting for the spot.

become unstable. This phenomenon is called ground effect. It adds extra lift, but the lift can be a bit rough.

In competitive hang gliding, ground effect is used to stretch the landing towards a bull's-eye target for extra points. As the target is approached, the nose of the glider is pushed upward very slowly and smoothly. At this point, the glider becomes a parachute, and the mind of the pilot must shift from that of a flyer to that of a parachutist; again, experience pays off.

In pleasure hang gliding, ground effect is used to stretch a flight to a safe landing spot. If, for instance, the landing target was cluttered with small jagged rocks that were not visible from the top of the cliffs, the smart pilot would pull up as much as possible, try to pick up some speed, and ride out the ground effect until he or she could land clear of the jagged rocks. A hang glider, when close to the ground, is, in fact, a kind of parachute; the glider itself is designed to stay aloft, but past a certain point, a landing is inevitable. Good parachute technique is valuable to pilots, and many hang glider pilots were originally parachute enthusiasts with many jumps to their credit. In any case, the goal of the Hang I rating is to achieve maximum control over straight-line flight. Radical banking, turns and other maneuvers should only be studied and not attempted until many ground-skimming hours have been logged.

Starting the stall.

Bleed-off for a stand-up landing using ground effect.

PSYCHOLOGY OF THE FIRST STAGE

As most pilots notice subtle changes in mood sometime during the basic ground-school training, it appears that growth in hang gliding is both mental and physical. Hang glider pilots are rated in five stages of growth, based on their degree of competence in the air. They also seem to evolve through five stages of consciousness. Support of this statement will appear as the entire field of hang gliding is explored in depth.

After Hang I training is completed, the pilot will notice a number of changes. The pilot will be in much better physical condition, and more importantly, the mental attitude will be improving. Research shows that anxiety and neurosis seem to melt away as hang gliding progress accelerates. Why this is so can only be speculation. From the psychoanalytical viewpoint, the awareness of freedom from an earth-bound existence, or at least the anticipation of such freedom, may create a deep subconscious transformation, perhaps even at a genetic level. In clinical terms, flight is an archetypical experience. Dreams of flight and the urge to fly are commonplace in every culture and every society. Throughout history, winged creatures appear in every mythology.

The Mayans and Aztecs worshipped the winged serpent Quetzalcoatl, and the Sumerians and Babylonians had a number of solar heroes who were at one time living priest-kings; they are depicted with wings on a number of frescos and carvings.

In South American jungles, certain witch doctors, called *Curenderos,* use a drug called *yage* to promote the sensation of flying. This drug, which contains harmaline, is made from the vine of a jungle plant called *caapi.* It is crushed, and then other herbs are added while it brews in huge tin cans for many days. After the liquid is consumed, the *Curendero* directs the drinker to dream, and, for some reason as yet unexplained, the dreams often entail flying.

In American children's literature, Maurice Sendak has portrayed the flight of a small boy during sleep. In this story, *The Night Kitchen,* Mickey flies naked from his bed to greet such characters as Laurel and Hardy in the sky. This book has helped children all over the world overcome their fears of dreams. Psychologists think that almost everyone has had a flying dream at some time.

Behavioral theory states that the only inborn fear is the fear of falling. Although this statement has not been fully proven, it is true that infants fear a sudden drop. In fact, a desire for security in infants might be ex-

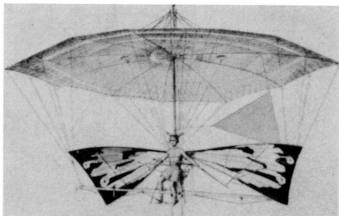

Letur parachute, 1853. This parachute was the direct result of experiments Leonardo's earlier work.

pressed as "Please don't drop me." Infants who were dropped or had similar experiences may have fears of flying as adults; these are sometimes the white-knuckled passengers whom we see in airplanes. That is not to say that all hang glider pilots are undropped babies; perhaps some hang glider pilots are trying to overcome insecurity. In any case, the psychological impact of flight on both the pilot and the public cannot be ignored.

The winged scorpion with the lion's head symbolizes the flight of the spirit . . . the quest for flight.

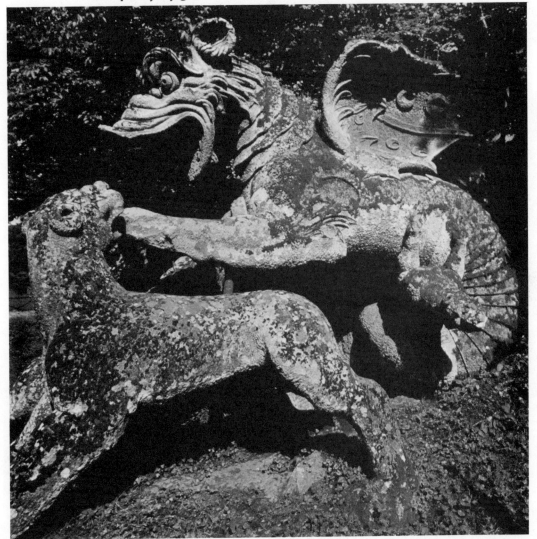

Father and son flying tandem, San Diego, California.

Bettina Gray

3

In Search of An Updraft: Advanced Flight

*A man in a flying machine must be free from the
waist up to be able to balance himself as one
does in a boat, in order that the center of
gravity of himself and of the machine may tilt
and change location when required to do so by
the change of the center of the resistance to it.*

Leonardo
"On the Flight of Birds"
Folio 5, recto
First Paragraph

At a hang gliding championship in Heavener, Oklahoma, a ten-year-old girl was observed taking her first gliding lesson. The harness barely fit her, and during this experience she was able to soar no longer than a few seconds, travel no more than three meters, and fly no more than one meter above the ground. Yet the throaty noises she made in that brief flight were not sounds children utter at school recesses while playing dodgeball. Instead, these were deep screams, complex yells, signals of great joy, great insight and marvelous fear, as if to say: "Oh! Now I understand what it's all about. . . . I'm on my own. I'm free!" This was a primal experience.

Arthur Janov, who has made a life study of human primal experiences, states that neurotic behavior is unintegrated behavior. By this Janov means that the two halves of the human brain do not interact or integrate in the neurotic personality; mental blocks have been inserted during early childhood. In the neurotic, the two cerebral hemispheres are out of sync and unbalanced. Hang gliding, more than any other sport, integrates brain function, relieves anxiety and tension, and removes mental blocks. In short, hang gliding tends to work toward the integration of consciousness. This is not to say that hang gliding is the cure-all for all psychosomatic distress, but the sport is therapeutic. A pioneer who gave his life to the sport of hang gliding said:

> Hang Gliding burns energy, a lot of mental and physical energy. It's a mind game with unknown and limitless rules. The further a pilot ventures into the unknown regions the greater the risk. At any time a new set of circumstances may appear that do not follow the rules of flight as known to the pilot. On these occasions, the pilot must be persistent, innovative and strive to regain full control of the situation. [Steve Spurlock, 1947–1976]

Gliding beginners are defined as those pilots who have confined their flights to a Class I hill, which is a hill with a vertical drop of no more than 20 meters. All beginner flights must be supervised and conducted below treetop level, preferably in areas with no trees and little or no turbulence. Beginning experience should be gained in different spots with slightly different conditions and with no crosswind surprises. No single launch hill can teach all that is necessary, and there is no substitute for experience.

To qualify for a Hang II rating, the pilot will have to make deliberate controlled turns and will have to fly more than 15 meters above the ground on a number of occasions. These maneuvers must be observed by a registered flight instructor.

THE 45° TURN—HANG II RATING

Reaching the Hang II level of proficiency is one of the most critical transitions in hang gliding training. From this point on, hang gliding is serious, and the 45° turn is the key to this rating. A minimum headwind of 25 kph is needed. Speed is critical here, because turns require slightly more speed than straight-line flight; turning a foot-launched glider increases the drag coefficient, thus slowing the glider and shortening the flight. Expert instructors state that crosswinds should be avoided in first-turn practices, but slight breezes always manage to pop up when they are least desirable.

The 45° turn seems simple, but even this maneuver requires a flight plan. The pilot should know the launch conditions, the turn direction (right or left), and the touchdown point. He or she should also be familiar with landing technique by this time, because the landing target as a point of mental focus is critical to any beginning turn practice. Both early and modern hang gliding pilots have observed that birds seem to focus their

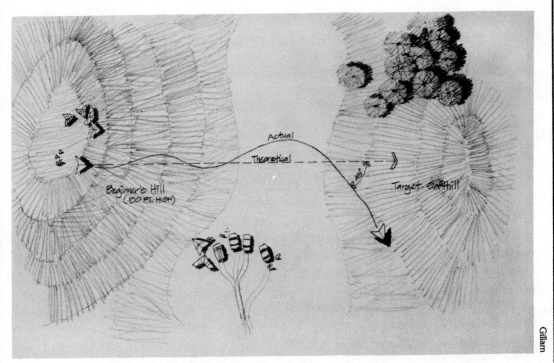

Beginners' hill, Hang II rating, stage one: The 45° turn.

attention on a given landing target before they execute their final turn.

If, when the pilot is attempting a 45° turn, the nose of the glider starts to move up or down too rapidly, a correction must be made. Instructors always insist that care be taken not to overcorrect with sudden moves; too much push will cause a stall-out which, even at a 20-meter height, can be very treacherous; in fact, most injuries take place in falls from 20 to 50 meters above ground, because a stall or dive may not be correctable in a short time. For Hang II rating, it is wiser and safer to turn in a slow wide arc, keeping the wings as level as possible—that is, with banks of less than five percent. In actual practice, true level flight is impossible, but level flight is the ideal.

The next progression for Hang II competence is another 45° turn in the opposite direction. Naturally, pilots must observe the same precautions as in the first turn. In hang gliding, as in motorized flight, all turns require some maneuvering; the nose must be pulled down slightly to gain speed, because the turn itself will cause a slight stall. However, radical banking tricks, such as wing-overs and loops, must be avoided until the more advanced maneuvers have been mastered.

A Hang II rating will also require a 90° turn, but United States Hang Gliding Association (U.S.H.G.A.) instructors allow the 90° turn only after the 45° turn has been perfected, since 90° turns require slightly more banking action and more speed. In any case, severe banking tilts of more than 10° are close to the limit of safety even for Hang III pilots, especially near ground level. Under international regulations, no one can proceed to a Hang III rating until the 45° and 90° turns are second nature.

THE CHICANE OR SLALOM TURN

The next maneuver necessary for a Hang II rating (and one that has proven extremely practicable in everyday pleasure flying) is the S-bend or Chicane turn. These slalom turns are theoretically simple, but require hours of safe practice. Basically, they are combinations of 45° turns which double into 90° turns, again with as little banking as possible. These are double-backs or zigzags performed in nonturbulent wind conditions from a 50-meter launch point.

The following list is a rough sketch of the requisite talents necessary for progressive hang glider control. The U.S.H.G.A. has a detailed formal list, but this list is designed to brief the nonflier:

I. The human body acts as a pendulum or drop line in hang gliding. As the body weight pendulates to the left, the glider flies to the left. So the pilot must learn to push the control bar in the direction opposite that of the body weight. The wing provides resistance, but the human muscles must push against this resistance to gain control.

II. The muscle-to-resistance control factor must be subtle and sure. This is a matter of muscle tone, knowledge of flight principles, and psychological preparedness. Overcontrol and overconfidence cause accidents. Hang gliding is basically gut-level noninstrument flying, although some instrumentation is available in more advanced practice.

III. In order to pick up flight signals, the pilot must tune in to the vital signs and sounds of hang gliding. If the sail is lufting (that is, flapping loudly) and the control bar is getting tough to push, the glider is probably exceeding its tolerance limits. Some modern Rogallo gliders can safely soar in a straight line above 30 kph, and fixed-wing gliders can make 50 kph under control. Therefore, as the pilot advances through the various hang glider ratings, acoustic signals become crucial, especially for thermaling.

The best way to judge speed is to listen to the wind. Excessive speed can be corrected only by pushing the nose up. Conversely, high altitude stalls can be avoided by fine control and by creating subtle dives which

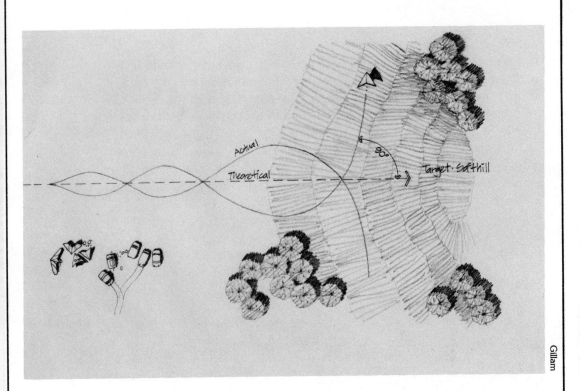

Gillam

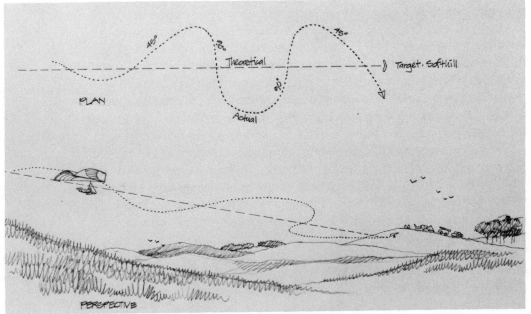

Gillam

Beginners' hill, Hang II rating, stage three: The slalom combination turn.

slightly increase speed. At normal flight speed, the glider should flutter lightly or remain quiet in still air. If the glider is dead silent and the control bar is not responsive, the glider is probably in a stall configuration. In this case, the control frame must be tucked in slightly. This should bring down the nose, and air speed should resume.

There are no horizon controls on hang gliders, so it is very easy for the pilot to become disoriented. This is why many hours must be spent in Hang I and Hang II practice before progressing to the more advanced levels. Advanced pilots all agree that air speed is nothing to fear. The higher the speed (within tolerance limits), the more efficient the operation of the hang glider becomes.

There is an irony in all of this. The great Leonardo da Vinci and Lilienthal and John Montgomery probably never exceeded a Hang I or Hang II rating. Despite all of their genius, they were basically alone in their research; they had access to a few basic ideas and perhaps some mythological stories that had been passed down to them, nothing more. In da Vinci's case, this was enough. Some ideas of Roger Bacon, some stories about the old flying masters, his mathematical ability, and his remarkable powers of observation gave him the desire to join the falcons and hawks, the bats and other flying animals. The question is, was Leonardo even a beginner? Did Leonardo fly?

LEONARDO DA VINCI ON THE ROAD TO HANG III

Some pilots think that Leonardo was really trying to revolutionize human consciousness by taking research a step further into practical application and by setting an example for the world, a world that is only now taking the first timid steps towards duplicating Leonardo's ideas.

Of course, there are reasons for the Leonardo lag—one of the most important being the fact that the Industrial Revolution stood in the way of individual development. Now people are getting a glimpse of Leonardo's true intention. Leonardo wanted all human beings to master the four elements if they could. And he would certainly be delighted to see hang glider pilots soaring with their multicolored kites above desert thermals and ridge lifts all around the world. Now almost anyone with courage and skill can experience flight and master the air, the second element in Leonardo's theory.

In "The Essay on the Flight of Birds," from the *Codex Atlanticus*, Leonardo proved that he had observed thermals, sink-rate, lift-to-drag ratio, wing loading and other basic aerodynamic factors, although he used different labels for them. In this regard, he conducted many experiments to

The urge to fly—to transcend the material plane—is so fundamental that it must be considered as primal as the urge to live. Lilienthal, Da Vinci, King Bladud of Bath, and Sinbad all had fantasies of flying. The South American drug yage—Bandsteriopsis Caapi—creates flying visions in almost all users; its ingredients harmala and harmaline are also found in the European plant wild rue. The Shamen of the Russian steppes report flying and levitation phenomena.

test the power requirements for human winged flight. At first, he assumed that a strong man would be able to flap a set of wings (the ornithopter concept) and also lock his arms to glide, but this was proven wrong by his own experiments and those of hundreds of others who came after him. No human being has the strength to flap a pair of wings and soar as the birds do.

Leonardo must have realized that humans are vast general-purpose machines, capable of a great many things; but evolution has traded off specialized adaptation for thinking and tool-making abilities. A biologically guided wing must be thought of as a tool, while a bird with hollow bones is a much more specialized creature. Naturally, both general and specialized creatures are only small parts of an even greater plan, and Leonardo knew this.

Da Vinci's second experimental series proved more fruitful. Here, Leonardo thought of the hang glider as a tool which he called *strumento*. In one experiment, Leonardo thought of flapping wings by turning cranks which would turn rudders in a rowboat with wings attached to either side. This led to the realization that the wings of birds are built to lock in place

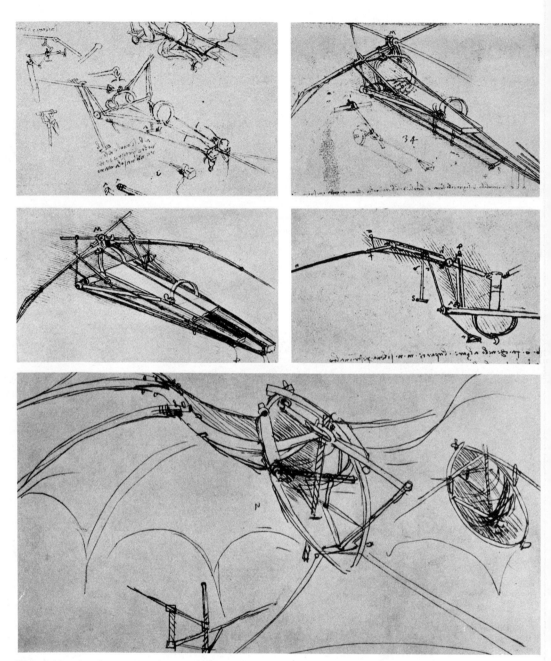

The flying boat was one of da Vinci's first experiments. Although it was a hopeless failure and was taken from the ideas of Roger Bacon, the medieval scholar, the research taught Leonardo a great deal about the nature of flight.

when soaring; thus, they become a single fixed wing under certain conditions. After studying bats, Leonardo clearly saw that he had to compromise and abandon the ornithopter idea. Flying, for the time being, had to be limited to soaring from cliffs on a bat-like wing covered with silk, hoping that an updraft could be located to stretch the flight a little further.

Like most Renaissance magi and alchemists, Leonardo thought of the world as composed of the four elements of the Zodiac—fire, air, earth and water. Each of these was multiplied by three, making twelve aspects altogether, the whole being the thirteenth. Leonardo called air the second element, claiming that it was the most difficult to master.

To Leonardo, the conquest of the second element did not mean a simple pencil-and-paper conquest. In the Renaissance, conquest meant personal baptism, personal trial, and direct confrontation. No scholar has ever proven that Leonardo actually flew his own wing, but a highly accurate documentary film, produced by the Italian government, implied that he did fly. It seems probable that Leonardo was adventurous enough to try his own wing after it was perfected. On this basis, it is reasonable to assume that Leonardo da Vinci did fly! In fact, hang gliding was undoubtedly Leonardo's true passion. It is the only single study that he carried on throughout his self-educated life. Painting and sketching were only tools for his massive genius. He studied architecture, anatomy, physiology, knots and mazes, optics, theology, military logistics and magic, but only flying research is woven throughout the entire body of his work.

Most hang glider pilots do not realize that Leonardo was not an isolated genius; he lived in a time of genius, when genius was respected (although ideas of social change were not). In his society, political manipulations were an art form, and genius was the fruit of good politics. Yet, in spite of his genius—or perhaps because of it—Leonardo was a pawn in the game of Renaissance social movements. Naturally, he was influenced by everything in his world, and his hang gliding research took a back seat to the planning of festivals, the designing of battlements, the painting of portraits, and those things that brought him income and patronage. Leonardo was a pagan magician in a Christian world, and his hang gliding ideas were stimulated by forerunners in his own neo-platonic tradition. Perhaps he knew of the work of Simon the Magician and King Bladud of Bath and was inspired by them.

Before the year 2000, someone will probably write a complete book on da Vinci's secret experiments, including his experiments with telescopes and alchemy, and his private observations on flight. Perhaps a heretofore unpublished manuscript will turn up from the dusty shelves of an obscure Spanish monastery, as happened with one of his sketchbooks. Until then hang gliding as an art form will proceed in his honor.

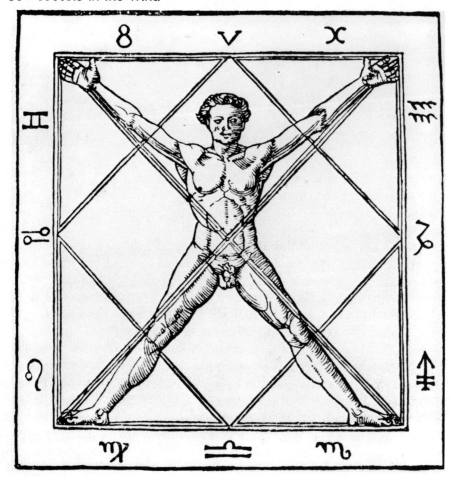

The Zodiac man of medieval astrology. This figure was based on the four elements: fire, air, earth and water. Da Vinci felt that by conquering the element of air in all of its complexity, human beings could someday fly.

LOOKING FORWARD TO ADVANCED HANG GLIDING

Leonardo probably never dreamed of *aluminum tubing* or a synthetic fiber made from petroleum, and he could never have thought of hang gliding as an international sport open to the participation of men and women equally. But he was aware that everything dangerous had to be mastered by degrees. This is why Leonardo would be proud of the modern hang gliding associations which teach hang gliding in stages.

The following is a list of factors that are clearly observable in Hang III- and Hang IV-rated pilots:

I. Physical condition: The majority of pilots engage in jogging, calisthenics and exercise to increase their control ability.

II. Diet: Almost all pilots in competition consider themselves athletes. They avoid junk food at all costs and properly analyze their individual needs for vitamin supplements and specialized foods.

III. Flight mechanics: Modern hang gliding pilots, without exception, possess a good working knowledge of flight mechanics and seat-of-the-pants flying.

IV. Meteorology and micrometeorology: An advanced hang glider pilot needs the same extremely keen knowledge of ecology, wind systems, meteorology, micrometeorology, clouds, and other factors that a regular motorized pilot or sailor must have. This knowledge has saved more lives than any advance in hardware and kite design.

V. Meditation and mental control: Most modern hang glider pilots study geography and geometry, and combine their pursuits with studies of ecology and psychology in an attempt to control and develop the mind.

THE TRUTH ABOUT ACCIDENTS

The U.S.H.G.A. has stated on numerous occasions that mechanical failures cause few injuries and fatalities in the sport of hang gliding, and even these few accidents are human in origin. In many cases, accidents attributed to mechanical failures, when investigated systematically, have turned out to be due to gross stupidity. Little mistakes, such as forgetting to hook the harness properly to the king post of the hang glider or flying with frayed lead wires, are classic stupidities. Some pilots fly with taped-up dacron or stripped bolts connected to control tensioners. These are not mechanical failures in the strict sense, for they could have been avoided. In most cases, the pre-flight check recommended by the U.S.H.G.A. was cursory or skipped. The major intent of the pre-flight inspection is to avoid accidents and thus promote hang gliding as a healthy, positive, albeit high-spirited, sport.

Unfortunately, no one can force a ding-bat pilot to replace a bolt or a wire on the spot; sometimes pilots are overenthusiastic. A mountain climber would certainly never attempt to climb a steep rock face with a frayed rope or worn carabiners; and scuba divers rarely exceed time-depth limitations in their dives. Yet untrained hang glider pilots sometimes fly with bad or borrowed equipment, and proceed with dangerous high frame-stress maneuvers, literally throwing caution to the winds. It is a wonder more fatal accidents do not occur, and it is this stupidity that originally gave the sport of hang gliding a sinister image.

A brief glance at the statistics may shed light on the safety of the sport. More than 200,000 safe flights are logged each year by pilots belonging to the U.S.H.G.A., to say nothing of the unlogged flights and the beginning practice flights. When viewed in this light, hang gliding is reasonably safe—at least as safe in proportion to the number of participants as is

ACCIDENT REPORT FORM

Complete and forward to USHGA, P.O. Box 66306, Los Angeles, CA 90066, immediately.

Date of Accident_____   Flyer's Name_____

Place of Accident_____   Flyer's Address_____

_____   _____
  Nearest City   State   City   and   State
Height of Hill_____   _____
Time of Accident_____A.M. _____P.M.   AGE   Phone Number
                                             Weather Conditions_____
Individuals who actually witnessed the   (Clear, fog, haze,...)
flight and/or impact (include address and   Wind speed estimate_____mph
phone number):_____   Gusty?_____Steady?_____
_____   Wind direction vs. flight direction:
_____   Directly into wind?_____
_____   Cross wind angle?_____

Experience of the flyer having accident_____
                                       (months, years, or # of flights) Badge rating?
Type of kite flown_____ _____
                  (Manufacturer)   (Keel length or type)
Type of suspension gear: Seat only_____ Prone harness_____ Combination_____

Protective gear worn by flyer: Helmet_____ Boots_____ Gloves_____ Other_____

Condition of kite after accident: Total wreck_____ Bent or broken leading edge_____
                                    Bent or broken control bar_____
                                    Torn sail_____ Bent keel_____ Other_____

Injuries: Fatal_____ Non-fatal_____
           Hospitalized overnight? Yes_____ No_____
           Head_____ Back_____ Legs_____ Arms_____ Other_____
           Describe apparent injuries_____
           _____
           _____

Describe flight and apparent cause of accident_____

_____

Other members of flying party who did not witness the accident itself (include address &
phone number):
_____
_____

Photographs taken by anyone at scene? Yes____ No____ If so, by whom? _____
Who has kite remains?_____

SUPPLY ANY OTHER PERTINENT INFORMATION ON REVERSE.
Please attach newspaper clippings or other data pertaining to accident.
Date of this report:_____   Name of Reporter_____
                                         Flying Experience_____
                                                   (mos., yrs., # flights)

snow skiing. Yet to some extent the public feels that hang gliding is as dangerous as snake bite: not always fatal, but ever painful. This fallacy must be reversed. There are a number of ways that hang gliding as a sport can be regulated, and there is no doubt that the federal government or some international council will eventually step in to regulate hang gliding activities if hang glider pilots, as a body, do not regulate themselves.

One method of regulation would be to adopt the same system that scuba diving associations have used over the years. They make sure that

Three altimeters and a wind speed indicator (lower right).

all manufacturers sell their equipment only through sanctioned outlets and that all outlet dealers sell equipment only to professionals, or at least highly skilled pilots who can show verification of their competence ratings. The U.S.H.G.A. has developed a special accident form that is distributed to all members, just as a log book is distributed to pilots and sailors. In fact, the accident form is part of an overall log-keeping duty that all pilots must perform. When these forms are collated, the U.S.H.G.A. can make stringent rules to correct weak spots and manufacturers' errors.

INSTRUMENTATION BASIC

In the primary grades, hang gliding needs very little instrumentation. A variometer, which records and feeds back the rate of climb and fall, is not really necessary until thermal soaring and cross-country flights are encountered at the Hang IV level of competence. In Hang II qualifications the most important gadget, next to a helmet and a safe harness, is the wind gauge, a device which tells the pilot the speed and direction of the wind both on the ground and in flight. After a few flights the pilot begins to sense the wind as if it were a real, living entity; the crosswind factors and the wind speed become second nature—the wind gauge is then used only to confirm the intuition.

Hang gliding must eventually become an automatic skill, like taking pictures with no light meter. All the pilot really needs to know is the exact nature and speed of the wind. One major role of the hang rating system is to teach the pilot the exact "goodness" or "badness" of the wind at any given time. Perhaps using the terms good and bad in this context seems a bit sophomoric, but hang glider pilots tend to use these terms to make judgments and their definitions seem to be based on survival.

The most important device used in hang gliding in addition to the wind gauge is an instrument known as a soaring variometer. The variometer can help in a critically rapid rise or fall situation. Should a pilot be sucked into a cloud or in some other manner deviate from sighting normal landmarks, he or she, through the use of the variometer, can learn the extent of the dive or the lift and thus reachieve level flight. A soaring variometer is an electronic, battery-operated device (although simpler versions do exist) which provides both audio and visual signals for the pilot. If a rapid rise in altitude is experienced, the noise of the variometer will rise in pitch and loudness. If a sudden drop is experienced, the variometer creates a noise that dips in pitch. A glance at the gauges will clarify the exact extent of this dive or rise.

Another device that seems almost essential for modern hang gliding is the airspeed indicator. For beginners, this little device helps develop speed judgment; and for intermediate pilots, the airspeed index helps when altitude renders ground-level indicators useless; both the variometer and the airspeed indicator are easily mounted on the framesupport struts within clear vision of the pilot of almost any hang glider.

A good healthy altimeter is also of great value. The altimeter is usually worn like a wristwatch next to the pilot's actual timepiece, which is, incidentally, another necessity. The altimeter apprises the pilot of his or her exact altitude above ground level.

The pioneers of hang gliding had no such devices. In fact, da Vinci did not bother to rig a proper harness, and Montgomery sat astride a wooden plank (rather uncomfortable, one would think). A variometer, in these cases, would have certainly helped; even the mythological Icarus would have been saved, because the variometer would have told him that he was soaring too near the sun and that his ascent was too rapid.

Other more complex instrumentation, especially for cross-country flying, will be discussed in the proper context. But the variometer, altimeter, wind indicator, chronograph and airspeed indicator constitute the basic lightweight instrument package for almost all intermediate hang gliding experiences.

Fog approaches Cerro Gordo.
Photo credit: George Harding

Sometimes, when there is no wind, people resort to all manner of tricks. This one is known as a head launch. Photo credit: Bettina Gray

Every hang gliding location has its own special way of transporting the hang gliders. This one is a trailer rig that can take about fifty gliders to the top of the mountain. Photo credit: Bettina Gray

Hang gliders are protected by special parachutes which save both the pilot and the glider. Photo credit: Bettina Gray

Retrieving a wounded hang glider. Mt. Cranmore, New Hampshire. Photo credit: Bettina Gray

Hang gliding is an open sport, a true democracy. Photo credit: Bettina Gray

Illegal glides down Half Dome are not rare. Yosemite National Park. Photo credit: George Armstrong

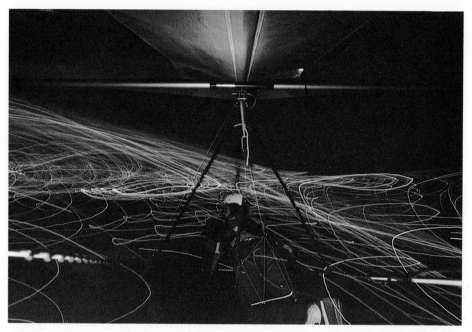

A rare night shot from a hang glider using a 20mm lens and long exposure.
Photo credit: George Harding

Cerro Gordo, level flight.

Cerro Gordo, right bank.

Cerro Gordo, wing over.
Photo credit: George Harding

The White Horse marks the site of an ancient Celtic hill fort in Wiltshire, England. It also provides excellent ridge lift. Photo credit: Harrison

Wind conditions can be erratic at Heavner, Oklahoma, but the total view is breathtaking. Photo credit: Harrison

"Up" is another word for hang gliding. Photo credit: Harrison

Balloons can often fly when hang gliders must wait for wind. Thus a natural affinity exists between the two technologies. Photo credit: Bettina Gray

Cape Cod is one of the original hang gliding locations in North America. This pilot seems a bit hung up after a safe crash. Photo credit: George Armstrong

St. Michael slays the Dragon. During the Dark Ages, St. Michael represented flight the way Thoth had earlier in Egypt.

In summer, ski tows make excellent hang glider lifts. Dog Mountain, Tennessee.

Bettina Gray

4

No Address On Cloud Street: Expert Flight

The great bird will take its first flight on the back of its great swan and filling the universe with amazement, filling all writings with its fame and eternal glory, return to the nest where it was born.

Leonardo
"On the Flight of Birds"
(back cover)

The Hang III rating is an intermediate pilot rating. Most Hang III pilots can soar and maneuver, but find it difficult to stay aloft for long periods in unstable conditions, because they have not developed the necessary skills. Achieving advanced and intermediate cross-country rating takes many hours, and no matter how expert a pilot becomes, the U.S.H.G.A. and international rating systems should not be short-circuited.

By the time the prospective pilot is ready to try for a Hang III rating, he or she will have spent more than $2,000 on equipment, including an advanced glider. The new high-performance glider will probably be more maneuverable and more stable than the basic trainer. It will offer a higher glide ratio, lower sink-rate characteristics, and better responses to the pilot's guidance. Along with the glider, the pilot will have purchased a special ear-hole helmet, a parachute, goggles, gloves, strong boots, thermal underwear, a flight suit, and a number of other devices used to refine the art of hang gliding.

ACHIEVING HANG III

The emphasis in Hang III instruction is on crosswind awareness and turbulence compensation techniques. In these flight situations, wind drift must be used to the advantage of the entire flight. In wind drift and crosswinds, a hang glider pilot must learn to crab—that is, pilot the wing sideways as well as forward. When crabbing, the nose of the glider seeks out and points into the crosswind, because the wing tips are twisted more than usual. The crosswind also creates a subtle vortex at the nose, which in turn creates a slight turbulence under the wing. This creates stall, which can be dangerous. Hang III pilots must be familiar with all of these factors and be efficient in reacting to them. Even a small vortex can cause a standard Rogallo glider to become unstable. To compensate for the lufting created by crosswinds, the Hang III pilot must use weight distribution properly. In sailboat navigation, this technique would be called tacking or upwind maneuvering. In hang gliding, the currents are much less predictable than in sailing, and micro-corrections must be made.

A Hang III rating also requires mastery of the 180° turn, including a reversal of direction. To perfect the 180°, a pilot must first make a 90° turn as soon as possible after takeoff. This puts the line of flight parallel to the takeoff point along the hilltop or ridge. After a parallel direction is established, a slight speed dive is started; at this point, a steady push on the bar carves the turn out, away from the hill. Now, being careful to avoid a stall, the pilot begins another turn parallel to the ridge, but in the opposite direction. The landing point can be either at a point below the ridge or, if there are no rotary winds, on top of the plateau. For the first flight, the pilot should plan to land at a lower level, but all turns must be made away from the launch point, away from the hill. Inward turns, occasionally lethal, are unnecessary gambles.

The final test for a Hang III rating is the figure-eight maneuver, but muscle control and flight awareness are also evaluated by the official examiner. The figure eight is also called the double-back S or Möbius turn. This is done by combining two 180° turns. The pilot plans the flight ahead of time, watches the wind conditions until the time is right, launches and proceeds to carve out a 90° turn. The pilot then continues this turn through an arc, repeats the 90° in the opposite direction, and lands at ground level. The flight path will have then covered a figure eight.

THE HANG IV RATING: SOARING

The Hang IV rating is only awarded after many months of figure eights, compensation control, 45° turns, 90° turns, slight banking maneuvers, figure S's, 360° turns extended like double 180° turns, and many safe landings. Actually, the Hang IV rating is based on the ability to gain

Hang III rating, stage one: Mastering the 180.

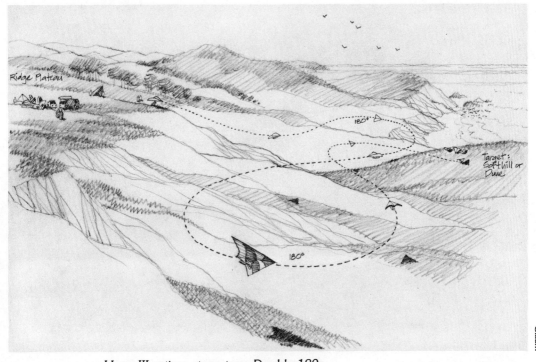

Hang III rating, stage two: Double 180s.

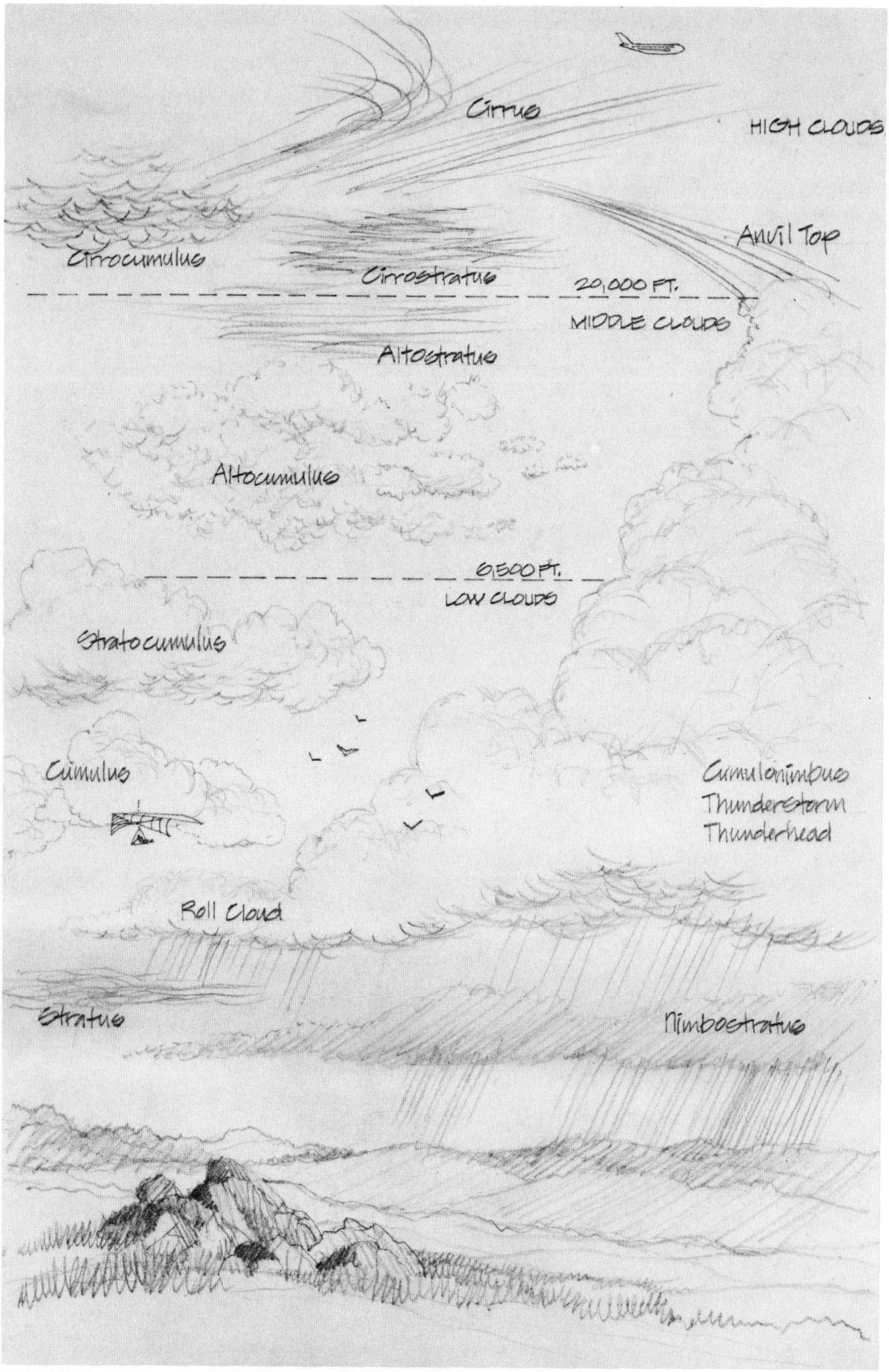

Cirrus

HIGH CLOUDS

Anvil Top

Cirrocumulus

Cirrostratus

20,000 FT.

MIDDLE CLOUDS

Altostratus

Altocumulus

6,500 FT.

LOW CLOUDS

Stratocumulus

Cumulus

Cumulonimbus
Thunderstorm
Thunderhead

Roll Cloud

Stratus

Nimbostratus

Gillam

The study of micrometeorology is essential for hang gliding competence.

altitude while combining all of the Hang III skills in any situation—and on logging many hours of flight time. Gaining altitude and holding it is the ultimate goal of hang gliding, because while soaring, the pilot can be totally alone with the elements for long periods of time. To do this, the natural sink-rate of the hang glider—that is, the tendency of any inert body to drop with gravity regardless of how efficient it may be—must be overcome by pilot skill. To soar, the pilot must guide the glider through various maneuvers in search of up-air, thermals and ridge lift. At Hang IV, soaring means staying aloft in all sorts of reasonable weather conditions, gliding long distances, maneuvering and landing safely.

SOARING THE CLOUD STREET

A long-distance flight along a cloud street is the ultimate challenge to Hang IV-rated pilots, but locating such a place is not simple. Cloud streets are formed when long stretches of fluffy white cumulus clouds develop in a straight line. A cloud street can extend for hundreds of miles, although most streets are shorter, and it is filled with soaring possibilities, including perfectly smooth winds sometimes called vespers. Unfortunately, cloud streets form only on special days and under rare meteorological conditions. In North America, they occur most frequently in the fall, most commonly over flat plains or deserts, and only occasionally over the ocean; so finding a cloud street usually means traveling inland.

In their most perfect version the streets almost always form on a hot sunny day immediately after a rain shower or light storm. In this situation, soaring visibility is unlimited, except for the dense clouds of the street itself. These clouds are called cumes or cu's (for cumulus) and are sometimes short-lived, especially when they overdevelop into anvil clouds or thunderheads. When the cumes are stable, they tend to drift with the breeze while maintaining their integrity for long periods. This makes them ideal for cross-country soaring; you just grab a cloud and drift with it.

Cumes are created indirectly by the sun. First, the sun heats the air in patches determined by ground contours. Trees and grassy fields retain heat and do not heat as fast as rocks. On the other hand, bare ground reflects heat. Thus, the hotter ground areas send invisible heat waves which move to a ceiling between 2,000 and 6,000 feet. The rising heat strikes the colder upper air, and a cloud forms from the condensation.

It is difficult to describe the experience of soaring along a cloud street at 3,000 feet, somehow melted into the weather, all the while knowing that mushrooms are growing in the woods below and that somewhere above a huge rainbow is beginning to spread like an arch. In this situation, cross-country soaring is achieved by hopping from cloud to cloud for as long as possible. The pilot must merge physically and psychologically with the environment. This is where both reserve stamina and the ability to meditate are of great merit.

Cross-country flying can mean flying hundreds of miles and can involve every known factor in hang gliding; beyond skill and awareness, the pilot must have the ability to fly without fatigue. Unlike sailplane flying, soaring for long distances is hard work; the pumping of adrenalin is almost constant and therefore exhausting. This is perhaps the greatest challenge in hang gliding—those who overcome fatigue and the other physiological variables can become record-breaking pilots.

When interviewed at Cerro Gordo in Southern California, where many distance records have been established, hang soaring pilots felt that someone will soar more than 500 kilometers some day. This may seem impossible, but some pilots predict that even longer flights will become commonplace, especially with motorized gliders.

AVOIDING THE ROTOR: RIDGE LIFT

The art of soaring is usually divided into two distinct studies—cliff soaring and thermal soaring—although in practice they are often encountered together. Cliff soaring is built around updraft ocean or desert winds. Smooth air usually comes across the ocean or desert floor at a constant low speed and eventually strikes a cliff or steep hill. As the wind continues to strike the bottom of the steep upgrade or cliff, a rotating turbulence is created. This bottom rotation then accelerates the wind up the sheer face, creating a vertical updraft which spreads out and smooths as it rises, the exact shape depending on the height and texture of the cliff. In other situations, the rotor at the bottom of the cliff may extend up the cliff edge, creating a dangerous condition referred to as boiling air.

Advanced hang glider pilots know that there are certain days when hang gliding cannot be practiced under any circumstances. Under borderline conditions, the pilots usually elect to send up what is ungraciously referred to as a wind dummy. This is an expert pilot who can report conditions to other pilots. If the wind dummy cannot fly safely, no one flies. When no wind dummy is available for competitive situations, smoke bombs are set off, and the smoke trail is carefully observed. When no smoke bombs are available, other reliable wind indicators must be used. In Wiltshire, England, at Aubrey Hill, a chimney from a local factory provides ample steam vapor six days a week.

Under ideal cliff-flying conditions, the vertical updraft remains stable as it breezes up the cliff face, but as the wind reaches the top edge, it starts to dissipate. Some of it shoots straight up and some twirls outward, depending upon the crosswind's downdrafts and its original velocity. Another portion of the wind separates and rotates back toward the plateau like a water fountain. Because of winds that originate inland, a vacuum can occur, and about a third of the up-air flow can be sucked back toward the open cliff top. This air can start to rotate, creating an unstable turbulence called a rotor. Quite often this rotating air, referred to as a hole in the wind, is very dangerous, and although rotors are not usually strong enough to tear a glider apart, they can dash a landing pilot to the ground before control compensations can be made.

Rotors are usually no problem until the pilot wishes to land. The pilot must pre-plan the flight so that the rotor is completely avoided on landing by choosing a spot well behind it. In case of rotors, all major instructors tell their students to shoot for a safe landing on the beach or at the base of

Aubrey's White Horse Hill, Aubrey, Wiltshire, England.

the cliff, assuming the tide is out and the base of the cliff is not too far away. It is better to haul the hang glider back up the cliff the hard way than to crash close to the parking lot.

THE THERMAL BUBBLE: HEAT LIFT

Basically, a thermal bubble is a brief blast or pop of warm air rising from a hot spot on the ground. If the bubbles continue in multiples, they tend to stand for long periods of time, especially when there is no crosswind. If this is the case, the thermal bubbles become columnar thermals. These thermal columns are often invisible and usually consist of smooth up-air, but like the desert dust devils (those small twisters that can be seen on dry windy days), thermals can be set into rotation.

If no damp air exists close to the ground and if the thermal is columnar, few clouds will form. Thus, the thermal will be virtually undetectable unless a few eagles or gulls happen to be hang gliding that day. The idea in hang gliding, then, is to develop an awareness of thermal systems and to learn to probe the air for these thermals with the nose and wing tips of the glider. No reliable instrument exists that can accurately detect an invisible thermal. Even advanced electronic instrumentation must be interpreted with skepticism. The seat of the pants is the state of the art in hang gliding, and human sensitivity will always be a factor in the sport. This means the pilot must learn the technique of instant thermal analysis simultaneously with all the other skills.

Thermals are not always safe. Sometimes they are big enough to have rotating holes in the center, just as if they were small cyclones. Because they are vacuous, these holes are often turbulent; so, for the sake of survival, a cross-country hang glider pilot must be more of a thermal expert than a sailplane pilot.

By now, it should be obvious that hang gliding is really bare-bones sailplane flying, in that many of the same principles apply to hang gliding, ballooning and sailplane flight. One end result of this advanced training in thermal reading is the ability to gain thousands of feet in altitude in a very short period of time. In 1976, a pilot stepped off a 2,000-foot ridge in Telluride, Colorado, caught a massive lift wind, and by skillful maneuvering soared the jet stream at 19,000 feet (approximately 7,000 meters). In the slang of the time, this was called a "sky-out," a term that seems self-explanatory.

The only problem with riding a thermal all the way to its top is getting back to earth. Only a pilot with a Hang IV rating will have the skills needed to get home safely, so no one with Hang III competence should

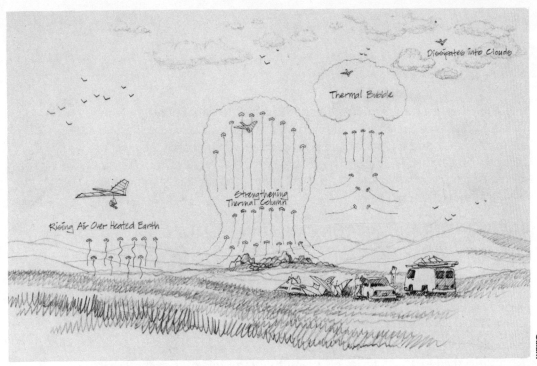

Hang glider pilots must study thermals and the use of updrafts in addition to micrometeorology and ecology.

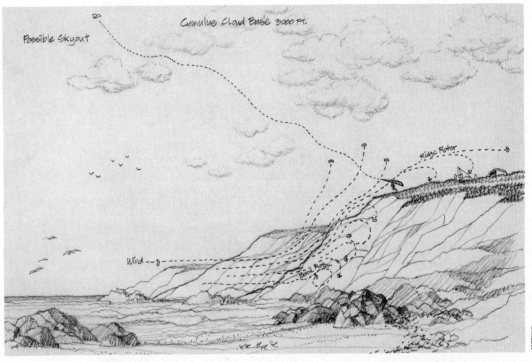

Ridge lift, wave formations, crosswinds and rotors can be helpful to the well-trained pilot and disastrous for the untrained.

ride a tall thermal bubble unless he or she wishes to gain an instant Hang IV rating and take the chance of injury in the process. Because thermals are as old as air and oxygen, there is an excellent chance that they will be around for a while. You can wager a safe and tidy sum that the sun manages to create a thermal somewhere every day; in short, some thermals just aren't flyable.

THE CONTINUING HISTORY OF HANG GLIDING

In addition to understanding the variables in the development of hang gliding competence, it is also important to understand the history and traditions of foot-launched flight. The popularity of hang gliding as a sport accelerated greatly in the early 1970s, but in the past no one knew anything about flight; most people deemed it virtually impossible and cared little for the ideas of da Vinci and the more ancient pioneers.

Da Vinci died in 1519. From his death to the middle of the nineteenth century, a span of almost 300 years, no one gave much thought to hang gliding or aviation. Even myths about winged animals and creatures from ancient civilizations were considered silly. During both the baroque period and the eighteenth century (the so-called Age of Enlightenment), cynicism took over. Most people were confused by everyday existence, let alone the rapid changes of the Industrial Revolution. The average human life was so arduous that little time was left over for thoughts of flight; only a few visionaries made contributions to the research. But the 300-year hiatus in aeronautics research and development was ended abruptly by an English country gentleman and scientist, Sir George Cayley.

Cayley was born in Scarborough, England, in 1773, a precocious youth with ideas of fantastic scientific experimentation. From the time he was very young, he was inspired by the vigor and insights of da Vinci and the other early scientific pioneers. Cayley lived 84 years, and his entire life was marked with great honors. He is even, on occasion, referred to as the father of modern aviation. (This title, although richly deserved, is a bit confusing, since Lilienthal and da Vinci are also referred to by that same title.)

Cayley held patents in technological areas as diverse as any polar opposites could be. He improved the telescope; he invented the first prosthetic limb, a workable false leg. He produced a caloric internal-combustion engine 100 years before anyone else, worked on a steam-powered robot with other advanced experimenters, and invented the caterpillar tractor. But this was only a start. Cayley also developed a

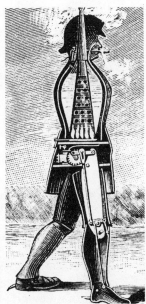

Robot man. Similar to that worked on by Cayley.

tensioner chain mechanism which is now used in all overhead cam engines, and he designed roadbeds for railroads. He dabbled in politics and worked as a landscape architect; in this context he created the allotment or "victory garden" which proved so useful to the Dutch and English in World War II. It is obvious that Cayley was ahead of his age. His only real contemporary was the Swedish genius Emanuel Swedenborg, founder of a mystical religion, who also designed wings. By modern standards, Cayley could have retired happily at age 35, since his life, by normal judgment, was complete. However, he remained scientifically active until after 1855, when he became a co-founder of the Regent Street Polytechnic Institute of London, a school designed to educate gifted generalists like himself.

In 1808, at the age of 35, Cayley was able to navigate a foot-launched hang glider with a wing surface of 300 square feet. This early glider weighed only 56 pounds and was tested with a dead weight of 84 pounds. At this weight, the glider could soar, but it had no harness and Cayley had no mind to fly the glider himself or even test it in actual flight. In 1848, forty years later, Cayley perfected a wing with a curved cross-section which utilized lift more effectively. For this contribution, he is more specifically known as the father of the modern airplane wing.

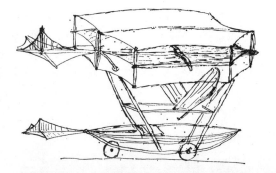
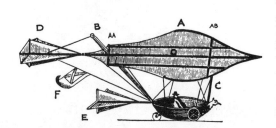
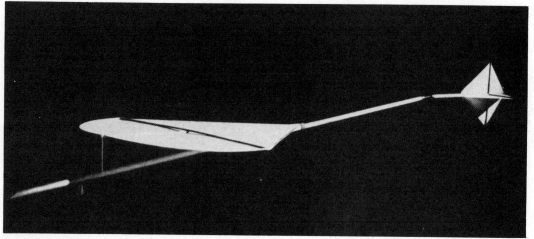

Cayley's gliders.

Cayley never stopped his explorations, but he continually came back to his beloved work—glider configurations. Cayley's most advanced glider design had both a wing and a tail which acted as a rudder. This plane had a larger wing surface than the earlier models, 500 square feet of combined area, and weighed 170 pounds loaded. On several occasions this one was flown for many meters by a ten-year-old boy strapped to a pine plank, but something was wrong. The glider was out of balance. As Cayley continued to work, he gradually improved the wings until certain of his own servants were willing to volunteer to be pilots.

On the first attempt, Cayley's coachman flew the big glider across a Yorkshire valley near Brompton Hall, Scarborough, Cayley's ancestral estate. And at least one of the coachman's experimental flights lasted many minutes and exceeded 1,500 feet (about 500 meters) in distance.

Unfortunately, Cayley's contemporaries would have thought him a bit addlebrained and possibly even accused him of delving into the occult if they had discovered the actual nature and extent of his hang gliding experimentation. Thus, Sir George was reluctant to report his findings to the Royal Academy, so it was many years after his death before his major contributions were discovered in his notebooks and sketches. In fact, Cayley would have avoided publication in any official form during his lifetime, if it had not been for a report that a Viennese man, Jacob Degen, had flown with wings under muscle power. This proved to be a fraud—most of Degen's weight was supported by helium balloons and the wings were used more or less for effect—but the report caused Cayley to publish his landmark paper titled "On Arial Navigation."* This paper details Cayley's experiments with the horizontal tail and vertical elevator which are the basis for all modern aircraft.

Unfortunately, the motors, stabilizers and curved wing sections that Cayley designed were not fully understood until the time of the Wright brothers. In fact, not until the 1930s were motorized aircraft able to take full advantage of Cayley's developments.

F. H. WENHAM AND A DOZEN PELICANS

Cayley was not completely alone. There were other pioneer explorers in the hang gliding field who may even have used some of Cayley's ideas covertly. Another Englishman, F. H. Wenham, who perhaps studied Cayley's work from a distance, observed pelicans in flight and noted two or more pelicans using the drafts of the birds beneath and above. This observation led to the development of wing drafting and to the invention of the bi-wing glider. Wenham's report to the Royal Aeronautical Society in 1866, nine years after Cayley's death, was a landmark paper which detailed a great many formulas for using curved cross-sections for greater lift and stability on both multiple- and single-wing gliders. In fact if it had not been for Wenham's historical contribution, Cayley's ideas might have died completely.

At the time Wenham gliders were causing a stir in England, a Frenchman named Mouillard was developing gliders in France and writing extensively about them. And another Frenchman, Alphonse Pénaud, was delighting children the world over with his toy gliders motorized by

---

* Sir George Cayley, "On Arial Navigation," in Nicholson's *Journal of Natural Philosophy, Chemistry and the Arts*, November, 1807; February, 1810; March, 1810.

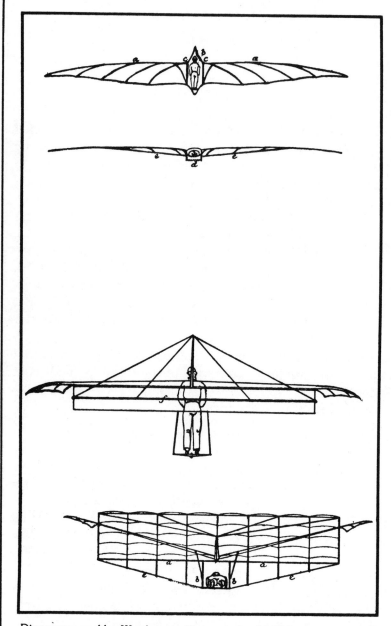

Diagrams used by Wenham to illustrate the 1866 lecture on the flight of pelicans and the use of multiple-wing surfaces.

twisted rubber bands. At least one of Pénaud's planes made its way to the United States, where it was employed by two young brothers, Orville and Wilbur Wright.

LOUIS PIERRE MOUILLARD AND THE NUBIAN VULTURES

Louis Pierre Mouillard published his first work in 1881. This exaggerated and highly publicized book, *The Empire of the Air,* greatly influ-

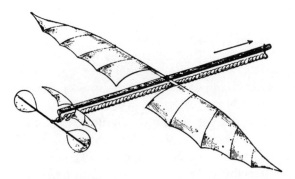

The "Planophore," 1871. In the early 1880s, the two young Wright brothers received a toy version of Pénaud's rubber-band plane as a Christmas gift.

Mouillard's illustration, from Historie de la Condor Nubian, *1881.*

enced H. G. Wells, Jules Verne, Otto and Gustav Lilienthal, and Arthur Conan Doyle. Needless to say, Mouillard was filled with the fervor of the *art nouveau* period and the movement of the Parisian artists of his time; as a result, Mouillard's book was a mishmash, virtually incomprehensible to all but a handful of enthusiasts.

On the other hand, Mouillard's work was not without a scientific basis. He did conduct observations of Nubian condors and Egyptian falcons near Cairo. Furthermore, while in Egypt, Mouillard attempted a few hang gliding experiments with his own glider. For his effort, he was awarded a great deal of acclaim in Europe, and, in 1897, applied for and was granted a U.S. patent. The model of his glider was exhibited in America at the World's Fair and at the Pacific Exhibition in San Francisco, but it was later destroyed. The present model on exhibit at the Museum of the Air in Paris is a reconstruction.

Mouillard's work—or at least his far-reaching ideas—had an impact on Americans as well as Europeans. The American hang gliding pioneer, John J. Montgomery, evidently attended the Pacific Exhibition and was fascinated by Mouillard's work.

MONTGOMERY VS. LILIENTHAL

For some as yet unexplained reason, international hang glider pilots pay homage to Leonardo da Vinci and Otto Lilienthal, but skip over the contributions of Cayley and John Montgomery. In fact, Montgomery had flown as high and as far at least ten years before Lilienthal. Lilienthal's flights took place in the 1890s in Germany, while Montgomery's persistent work, in both southern and northern California, covered a span of six decades; but only Lilienthal had the eyes of the world upon him.

Because of his talent in public relations, Lilienthal's contributions were considered chic, while world opinion held that Montgomery's work was the rambling of a thrill-crazed cowboy from California. This was unfair; like Lilienthal, Montgomery was a true aeronaut and his contribution should not be diminished.

It may be of some value to compare Lilienthal's and Montgomery's contributions. Lilienthal's work is summarized in his own book, *Bird*

(Courtesy Smithsonian Institution)

Otto Lilienthal in his bat-wing hang glider.

Lilienthal poses with his bi-winged glider next to his manmade launch hill.

(Courtesy Smithsonian Institution)

Peter Vischer the Younger: Fortuna Amoris. *Lilienthal postulated a concept that he called negative drag, an absurd unworkable idea which actually received some attention from the German scientific community of the time. This illustration from the Erlanger University library demonstrates the same principle. The drawing shows an angel vainly attempting to propel the globe forward by blowing on a sail.*

Flight as the Basis for Aviation, in which he speculates on the use of updrafts and thermals and postulates that a curved wing surface would provide more efficient lift than a flat surface. It is, however, a bit disillusioning to discover that both of these ideas were set forth separately in differing but accurate terms by Cayley and da Vinci.

Lilienthal then went into the absurd by postulating that certain wings could force themselves forward by means of a hypothetical force which he called negative drag. This would be similar to a sailor's blowing into his own sail. Negative drag is not only a semantic contradiction; it is also a physical impossibility. Lilienthal's theory of negative drag—in essence the same as the theories of levitation and anti-gravity—defied the laws of physics. In aviation, there is no such thing as positive or negative drag, only a drag coefficient. In fact, the idea is so weird as to cast doubt on the clarity of Lilienthal's thinking.

All of this simply means that Lilienthal, for the most part, was a thrill-seeking impassioned adventurer and eccentric who took the time to be nice to people. No doubt he was a genius, but it is difficult to consider Lilienthal's work totally original. Lilienthal's fame arose because he was in the right place at the right time, he was extremely persistent, and he engaged in thousands of flights in many parts of Europe, thus stimulating Chanute in America, Percy Pilcher in England, and eventually the Wright brothers.

John Montgomery lived in Santa Clara, California, and flew only in San Diego, Santa Cruz and the Santa Clara Valley. This was an obscure area with very little publicity available. He was certainly not in the center of the great cultural milieu of Europe; but obscurity may have helped Montgomery, who worked alone and unimpeded. In spite of Montgomery's obscurity, Thomas Edison took great interest in his work, as did Leland Stanford, the founder of Stanford University; and through Stanford, the military became interested.

In 1893, Montgomery met Octave Chanute, with whom he then began to correspond. He also gave a report at a Chicago convention proving that moving air deflects upward in front of the wing long before the current actually touches the wing edge. This was a critical, original and well-written paper, typical of his correspondence and research. It was significant in the development of fixed-wing, power-driven aircraft, and backed by solid, rigorous scientific method. It is also significant that Montgomery never gave up his work on flight in spite of discouragement and lack of funds. Montgomery, who held a Ph.D. from the University of San Francisco, patented a gyroscope which is on view at the Library of the Santa Clara University. A film of Montgomery's life, *Gallant Journey*, starring Glenn Ford, was made in 1946, but the film, like Montgomery's contribution to hang gliding, has been almost forgotten.

Lilienthal and Montgomery continued to work separately and relentlessly, but Lilienthal got most of the credit. Lilienthal was considered a sophisticated European by eastern American scientists, especially by S. P. Langley, the Secretary of the Smithsonian Institute, and by the military. Montgomery was considered a reckless stunt man, and his entou-

Glenn Ford and Janet Blair as Mr. and Mrs. John Montgomery in Gallant Journey—1946. Glenn Ford makes final adjustments to the Evergreen glider. Unlike the true story, the Hollywood version of John Montgomery's life had a happy ending.

rage received a bad press image when he put on shows at county fairs and other events to raise money for more experiments. Only within a small circle of the avant-garde on the West Coast was Montgomery's research and Yankee ingenuity acclaimed. Montgomery died in a crash when a lug bolt from his hang glider *Evergreen* pierced his skull (he flew with no helmet). But his contributions to hang gliding research were important, and they must be held at least equivalent to Lilienthal's.

Ironically, it was Lilienthal who had the last word (he too died in a hang gliding accident), even though he died long before Montgomery. On his deathbed, Lilienthal mumbled, "Sacrifices must be made." Lilienthal's last words, like his entire attitude toward the art of hang gliding, are open to criticism. Sacrifices, especially human sacrifices, need not be made. Da Vinci did not sacrifice himself, nor did Sir George Cayley, the Wright brothers, Octave Chanute or many other pioneers.

Lilienthal transporting his collapsible wing.

The spirit of the pioneers is still alive in hang gliding.

Bettina Gray

5

On the Wings Of Hawks and Doves: Professional Flight

The movement of the human-bird should always be above the clouds so as not to wet the wing and to survey more country, and to avoid the dangerous gusts of winds within the mountain passes which are always full of turbulence. If the bird be turned upside down you will have plenty of time to right it according to the directions already given, before it falls to the ground.

Leonardo
"On the Flight of Birds"
Folio 6, verso
First Paragraph

While Lilienthal and Montgomery were successfully experimenting with the hang glider, other groups of experimenters were toying with other ideas based on da Vinci's sketches. The two most important ideas became known as the ornithopter and the man-lifter. Contributions from both of these ideas appear in modified form in modern hang gliding. Thus, it is worthwhile to trace them briefly.

THE ORNITHOPTER

The ornithopter is a device that flies, or attempts to fly, by a wing-flapping or wind-screw technique. Many so-called fools, including da Vinci, tried to fly by this method, but it just will not work. Humans cannot fly by flapping sets of artificial wings strapped to their arms. Gliding is possible, but flapping the arms is absurd. Still, the deep-seated idea of self-propelled flight can become a reality if the pilot uses a bicycle or

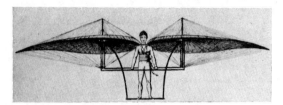

Degen's ornithopter design, 1809.

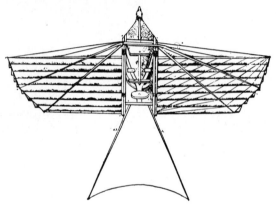

Walker's ornithopter design, 1810.

some other smooth-ratio mechanical apparatus as an interface device. The mechanics are necessary to magnify human body movements enough to overcome the weight of the pilot and the pay load. Da Vinci eventually realized the error of his ways and shifted his attention to the hang glider, but others who came later saw merit in the idea and continued to work toward the motorization of the ornithopter concept. This then became the helicopter.

THE MAN-LIFTER

The idea of lifting a human being in a kite may be very old. In fact, it is possible that the concept of using kite flying to lift a human being evolved as early as the Stone Age. It is known that Australian aborigines and the tribes of Borneo and Micronesia flew large bamboo and mat kites, and the Chinese used kites of ancient design, capable of lifting huge pay loads, during the Boxer Rebellion. Called Wan-Wan kites, they required many coolies to launch. The Wan-Wans are noted in Chinese folklore as having been used in the Tang Dynasty, one of the golden ages of Chinese antiquity.

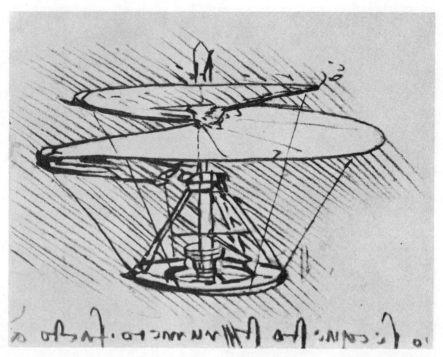

Da Vinci's air screw, which evolved into the helicopter.

In 1894, while Lilienthal was gliding in Germany, an Englishman named Lord Baden-Powell began adapting the Chinese Wan-Wan concept to Western uses. His research resulted in a man-lifter which could raise a soldier or observer from the ground rather nicely. Baden-Powell's kite looked uncannily like the parabolic kites developed by Dr. Francis Rogallo after World War II, but his was not a rigid soaring device.

To further the idea of the usefulness of the man-lifter, John Nicoliadis, a scientist working in the 1970s in California, designed a motorized parachute or "parafoil" kite. This kite was really a square-cut parachute with strong suspension cables attached. It was powered by a 25-horsepower snowmobile engine, but many other motors were substituted. The motor and pilot were suspended in a wheeled frame constructed of lightweight steel tubing, and the vehicle was pushed forward by a rear-mounted propeller. As the vehicle gained forward motion, the kite, which fit completely into a 60-litre plastic garbage can, filled with air, lifting the entire vehicle and pilot above the ground. Both climb rate and forward motion were regulated by the simple throttle control. Side motions and turns were controlled by straps attached to the pilot's harness.

Chinese Wan-Wan, or man-lifter kite. This device was prominent in the Boxer Rebellion and required dozens of workers to launch.

These two kite designs changed the history of flight. To the right, Lord Baden-Powell's man-lifter, 1894. To the left, Rogallo's flex-wing kite, flown in the 1960s by NASA scientists.

Lord Baden-Powell actually tries his own invention.

But what does all of this mean? What practical purpose could a man-lifter serve?

Warfare seems to be the prime mover in the application of any and all aircraft. After centuries of being used as a simple transport device on pleasure craft, the Chinese Wan-Wan was used to spy and to drop hand bombs. But Dr. Nicoliadis's motorized parafoil may yet be used as a recovery device for unexploded cruise missiles, as a remote pilotless vehicle (RPV) vis-à-vis a drone, or even as a temporary radio aerial for surveillance over the horizon, for the parafoil has been flown successfully up to two miles above the earth's surface.

Obviously, the man-lifter and the ornithopter are not directly relevant to the study of hang gliders. But it is also obvious that both of these ideas played an important role in the development of the technology of the foot-launched hang glider.

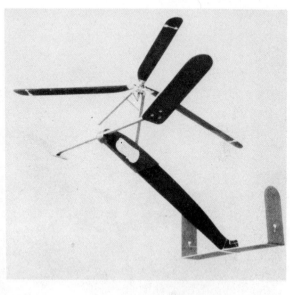

German navy testing gyro-kite in Second World War; this device is similar to a parafoil in some ways.

PERCY PILCHER

Powered flight was first conceived of in the Middle Ages by Roger Bacon, and the concept was further developed in the eighteenth century by Emanuel Swedenborg. But nineteenth-century power plants, mostly steam-driven models, were far too heavy for the light glider frames of Cayley, Lilienthal and Montgomery. For the most part, the dream of powered flight would have to wait until a stronger airframe structure was engineered. Steam as an energy source was effective for heavy machinery and ocean ships, but not for aircraft. The motorized planes of that era were drawing-board gliders, dream machines, fantasies. But at each step in the development of the glider, many experimenters made headway. The history of hang gliding is really a history of human creativity and technical problem solving. One roadblock would give way to an advance in another area of endeavor. Lucky, or in some cases unlucky, accidents

The Hawk, *built and flown by Percy Pilcher in England about the turn of the century.*

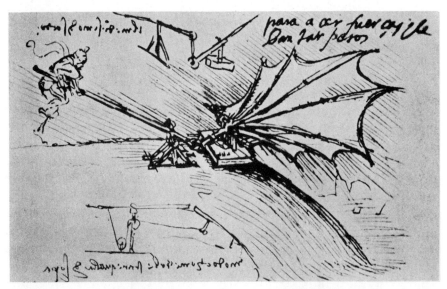

Da Vinci's ornithopter experiment to test the strength of a human muscle when lifting a wing.

always seemed to pave the road to future progress. Percy Pilcher is a good case in point.

At the age of 13, Pilcher began to dream of flight as a reality. His dream grew into the obsession that devoured his entire life. But Pilcher's research was not a waste; he came closer to powered flight than any other European and would have bested the Wright brothers by a number of years if he had not died in an accident in 1899.

After long study and a stint in the Royal British Navy, Pilcher attended the University of London and emerged a full-fledged engineer. From London, he proceeded to Glasgow to lecture at the university and to begin his experiments with hang gliders. Pilcher had little to go on except the studies of a few predecessors and good old British toughness.

In January, 1893, Pilcher built the glider he called *The Bat*. Its body was about 12 feet long and 2 1/2 feet wide. This glider boasted a wing loading of 1/2 square foot to the half-kilo, which enabled it to haul 80 to 90 kilos. But, in spite of this wing loading, Pilcher designed the glider to fold like an accordian. Lilienthal's glider also was designed in this manner, as are modern hang gliders.

On his first flight over Cardcross, Pilcher flew four meters above the ground and, much to his amazement, stayed aloft on a ridge lift for almost 15 minutes. This frightened him because he had scant means of control. Thus, his second glider incorporated more aerodynamic leading edges and wing tips. These modifications made it easier to land the glider at will.

Because he was a visionary who had visited Lilienthal in Germany and had flown in Lilienthal's kites, Pilcher wanted very much to use the calorific engine designed in 1809 by Cayley. But these engines proved impractical, as they set up a great deal of vibration. Pilcher was forced to develop his own engine, a light oil-burning model, based on the 1860 gasoline engine of the Frenchman Lenoir. In order to add this engine, Pilcher had to design a larger glider he called *The Hawk*. This glider retained the wheels and the towline takeoff techniques used with *The Bat,* but was otherwise quite different.

The Hawk was a very maneuverable craft, capable of soaring up to 250 feet, while gliding against headwinds, for more than 100 meters. Unfortunately, Pilcher crashed as he was testing this new design, and his research had very little impact on world aviation. Like Montgomery, who was working wonders in California at this same time, Pilcher was a media-isolate, more or less blacked out by the mainstream British and world press. It is sad to report that after Pilcher's death, practical efforts in British

Lenoir's gas engine, 1840. This engine was a prototype of one that was to be mounted on Percy Pilcher's Hawk. It is obvious that some miniaturization would be needed.

aviation virtually came to a halt. More than a decade would pass before the British would again begin experimenting with the designs of Cayley and Pilcher for use in World War I planes. Lilienthal captured all of the world's attention for twenty years, and only the Wright brothers could bring the limelight to the English-speaking world.

OCTAVE CHANUTE

In 1896, while John Montgomery was at work in California, Octave Chanute, another pioneer, was working on a stabilizing device or tail regulator called an automatic regulator, which allowed the wing to lean over in order to stabilize, thus rendering the glider much more stable. With it Chanute finally was able to prove that a bi-plane could be stabilized and kept from stalling.

In the same year, Chanute developed a full-scale flying glider which had six separate wing surfaces and a tail; actually, he used twelve separate sections set in six planes. With this design Chanute, a safety enthusiast, made more than 200 flights, while his assistant made a like number, all without difficulty or mishap. True, these jumps lasted only a few minutes and were never longer than 30 meters in length, but Chanute, working on the dunes along the shores of Lake Michigan near Chicago, proved that hang gliders were safe.

Chanute also stated quite emphatically that all flight experiments must be:

. . . worked out in a full size apparatus, mounted by a human being and exposed to the vicissitudes of the wind before any attempt is made to soar or to apply a motor or propelling device.

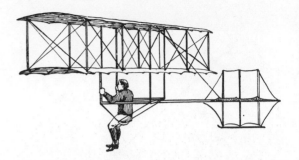

Gallaudet laterally controlled his glider (1898) using warping techniques that are still used in hang gliders today.

Chanute developed a hanging seat for his hang glider, using da Vinci's pendulum idea. This harness seat enabled him to change the direction of the machine while coasting by shifting his weight, something Lilienthal did by dangling his legs and leaning on his arms.

By the time 1902 rolled around, Chanute was on fire with the idea of flight, and, through correspondence with Montgomery and the Wright brothers, who had developed wing-twisting controls, he developed a tri-winged glider which was perfected by Chanute's assistant, a man named Herring. With the new machines, both bi-wing and tri-wing models achieved a distance of 100 meters or more and flew 10 meters above the ground. Unfortunately, these designs outperformed expectations, and a few of the flights ended in Lake Michigan, but no one was ever injured. At the peak of his experimental success, Chanute wrote a book entitled *Progress in Flying Machines,* which is now in the archives of the Smithsonian Institute in Washington, D.C.

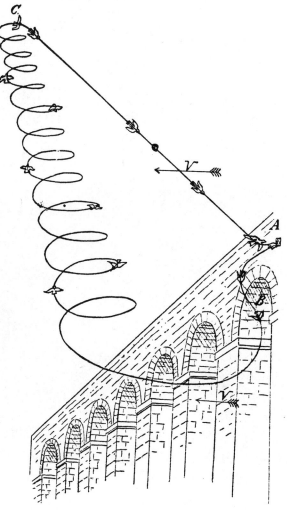

Chanute wrote a book entitled Progress in Flying Machines. *In it he described the spiral excursion of the sparrow hawk. The bird ascended in a narrowing spiral.*

THE WRIGHT BROTHERS

The success of Orville and Wilbur Wright's motorized flight in 1903 is common history, but few people realize that the Wrights had corresponded with Chanute, Mouillard, Lilienthal and Montgomery. Taking Chanute's ideas as a starting point, the Wrights began to design gliders which actually used controlled surfaces for better stability.

The first unmanned glider was launched in 1900, and the first manned flight in 1901. The earlier machine had a wingspan of 22 feet and an area of 290 square feet. This was a big plane by nineteenth-century standards, and journalists and scientists began to notice the Wrights' work.

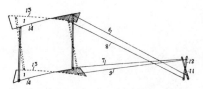

A. Wright biplane kite (shown without the tailplane-cum-elevator): 1899

B. Wright No. 1 glider: 1900

C. Wright No. 2 glider: 1901

The Wright brothers.

The Wrights' 1901 glider could support the weight of a human in mild wind and had excellent soaring capabilities. It was controlled by various tensioner cables which changed the shape of the wing by warping it. This warping technique gave good control stability against drift, thus helping the glider to maintain a straight line, while the forward elevator could be moved up and down to control lift. This same warping technique is used in modern hang gliders, both the single-wings and the bi-wings. Even some modified delta wings have slight leading-edge tension controls.

In 1902, working in the family bicycle shop in Dayton, Ohio, Orville Wright designed one of the first wind tunnels. Only 6 feet long, it still proved effective for experimental work with wing models. A fan mounted at one end of a box produced very little velocity, yet the Wright brothers abstracted more than 200 designs using only this tunnel. During this same period, Orville also designed and built a small engine which was

E. Launching the Wright No. 3 glider (modified), Orville piloting: 1902

eventually attached to an improved glider. This was the engine that made the first powered flights possible.

With the data obtained from wind-tunnel tests, the Wright brothers built their final glider. The new design made hundreds of safe unpowered flights in winds above 25 miles per hour. The improved 1902 model was often flown 10 meters above the dunes of Kitty Hawk, North Carolina, for more than 200 meters in distance. Bolting the engine on was simply an exercise; the glider was the major improvement. But the glider soon became the abandoned child of history. On December 17, 1903, the Wrights became immortal. Ironically, their powered flight was much shorter than their earlier glider flights—but who cared? The motorized glider made a world war possible!

THE WRIGHT BROTHERS AT THE GATES OF HELL

The First World War accelerated the need for superior weapons. The reconnaissance balloon was at first used in trench warfare, but bi-winged planes, even the earliest models, and the field radio made the balloon an outmoded jumbo. Trench warfare was dependent on the digging in of troops in long, narrow trenches. The troops attacked the trenches until one side or both were destroyed. To accelerate this destruction, weapons such as mustard gas and highly accurate mortars began to appear. Then the airplane was invented. The airplane was a major cause of the war. Anyone making a simple historical study can plainly see that the generals on both sides were so eager to use this new toy against the trench soldiers that they could hardly wait to start a war. These early planes may have been Putt-Putts, but they were lethal.

In 1910, some clever "dickey" invented a propeller cam device that allowed the machine gun to fire only when the propeller was parallel to the wings. With the help of this device, pilots delighted in dog fighting, shooting down balloons and strafing the soldiers in the trenches. This was a highly mechanized war, an aerial war, the first one of its kind in human history, and much of it, whether they intended it or not, hinged on the invention of Orville and Wilbur Wright, the two prodigious shade-tree inventors from Ohio.

Bird man with aluminum beak attempts to threaten a bemused spectator.

Harrison

6

The Hole In the Sky: The Future

*But you who live on dreams, you are better
pleased with the frauds of talkers about
great and uncertain matters than those who
speak of certain and natural matters not of
such lofty nature.*

*Leonardo
"On the Flight of Birds"
Folio 10, recto
Margin note*

The experience of being swept into the heavens on the wind is at least as old as the Book of Kings wherein . . .

> Elijah went up by a whirlwind into heaven. And Elisha [his successor] saw it, and he cried . . . and . . . saw him no more. [2 Kings 2:11-12]

In a similar way the twentieth century began with a whirlwind and everyone was somehow involved in flight—it took off with the Wright brothers and will end with the coming of age of hang gliding. Only since the 1960s have aviators realized their debt to foot-launched flight, and only in the latter third of the twentieth century have human beings been able to fly almost at will, thanks to hang gliding technology.

When World War I finally drew to a finish, Germany was placed under strict military and economic rules, but foot-launched wings and soaring gliders were harmless and inexpensive. This created a new group of flying enthusiasts who were dedicated to developing soaring and foot-launched gliding research. Like Wernher von Braun's rocketry group, few of these early aeronauts had any notion of National Socialism, and few could have

A Luftwaffe sailplane soars New York City, June 17, 1937. This curious feat was performed in a handmade Rhoneperber, *a prototype of later fighters. The pilot was Peter Riedel. Note the swastika on the tail.*

predicted the rise of Nazism, Hitler or the Second World War. But many early foot-launched pilots were German nationals, and they did have the private blessings of the newly formed German government.

Willy Pelzner was the most outstanding of these German aeronauts. From 1918 to 1921, Pelzner flew a double paper-winged hang glider that was small enough to be carried in a large suitcase. This glider boasted a glide ratio of about 6 to 1; this meant the glider could fly 6 meters forward for every 1 meter it dropped—not bad for a portable! For over a decade, the German competitions grew in size and popularity, combining foot-launched *Stormzeilen* with full sailplane soaring in towable aircraft like the *Blau Maus* or the *Schwarze Tauffel*. Hundreds of picnickers came to

Lange

In this well-balanced glider, the student frees the stick, and it flies alone. The framework of the Zögling, or pupil glider, was composed of steel tubes. The span of its wings was 33 feet. The glider without its pilot weighed approximately 200 pounds. Germany, 1931.

admire the sailplanes and the aerobatics of the hang glider pilots, just as crowds gather at present-day hang gliding competitions.

Adolf Hitler began attending these picnics in 1935 and took an enormous interest in things aviational. He was usually attended at these affairs by Hermann Göring and an entourage of twenty or thirty members of the New Reich higher echelon, including a famous aviatrix named Hannah Reitsch. Frau Reitsch finally convinced Hitler that fixed-wing gliders could be developed into weapons for silent attacks. Apparently, the hang gliders had been built as novelties, but Hitler was interested in Reitsch's suggestion because, for the most part, the German air force was limited by the treaty of Versailles, which forbade the motorization of any aircraft whatsoever. Obviously, Hitler fully intended to violate that treaty in the future.

Hannah Reitsch in a Zögling training glider, 1931. This woman was instrumental in the planning of the German Glider Air Force and went on to become a high-ranking air ace in World War II.

In 1930, Hermann Göring ordered a famous World War I flyer named Karl Student, an associate of the late Baron Von Richtoffen, the Red Baron, to organize a close study of the possibility of using sailplanes for silent warfare (ignoring hang gliders). Gen. Student visited the Soviet Union and observed Russian paratroopers leaping from sailplanes. He also trained German sailplane pilots on Russian airfields. Student's letters to Hitler motivated a great deal of secret activity, which would eventually develop into an attack on the Dutch frontier at the so-called impregnable fortress of Eben Emael. Student's final report stated that sailplanes were necessary because massive forts such as Eben Emael were protected by sensitive noise alarms that would note the approach of any motorized aircraft.

In 1938, after long preparations, the first phase of the *Luftwaffe* was born. The foot-launched hang glider had been set aside in favor of fixed-wing aircraft designated as DFS 230s. These wooden planes, carrying attack teams and explosives experts, could be towed and released, moving into the noise sensor area without detection.

Eben Emael was not only huge, it was also fortified with massive anti-aircraft and long-range cannons and was manned by the best troops in the Dutch and Belgian armies. Unfortunately, none of the builders of Eben Emael had thought of the possibility of a silent attack. This oversight enabled the gliders to spot-land on the roof of the fort, which was actually a huge grassy expanse covering a cement and steel bunker. From there, it was a simple matter of detonating gas bombs and huge explosive devices. Eben Emael fell in two days' time, and the second air war in Europe had begun. Hitler used this successful glider attack for propaganda and to show off his organizational skills.

As early as 1921, many European visionary pilots were following the foot-launched sky trails of Willy Pelzner and Otto and Gustav Lilienthal. At first, the hang glider group was small (a group of pilots left hang gliding to get involved in the *Wehrmacht* and the romance of the war-oriented sailplanes), but hang gliding was growing in size and technical know-how when interrupted by the war. At present, this group of peace-loving pilots is reemerging. Austrian pilots have developed safety devices which can prevent crash dives, and almost every day someone flies a hang glider over Lake Lucerne, near Geneva, Switzerland. The weather is too often perfect and the ridge lift in the Alps too solid to let a little thing like a war crimp the progress of a good idea.

FRANCIS ROGALLO AND THE POSTWAR DELTA WING

In America, immediately after World War II, a new generation of sailplane pilots soared for the fun of it as often as they could, but the foot-launched glider was all but forgotten. For some reason, apart from the obvious dangers and seeming craziness of it, the development of foot-launched flight was stalled in a technological vacuum. This vacuum was broken by Dr. Francis Rogallo, who developed and patented the basic ideas for the delta-wing kites which were later adapted into hang gliders. Like many aviation inventors, Rogallo was a dreamer as a child. His entire youth was dedicated to flying and the study of flight. An accident barred him from the air force in World War II, so he went on to advanced university studies. Ironically, avoiding the war may have influenced his attitude toward aircraft design, because his later inventions showed scant promise of military application.

NASA

Rogallo test-bed vehicle. NASA-Mars experimental prototype.

John Fairfax & Sons, Ltd.

Rogallo flex-wing as water-ski kite near Coral Gables, Florida.

In 1946, Rogallo went to work for the Piper Company in Pennsylvania. Because the Piper Cub had been used extensively for reconnaissance work in both war theaters, the Piper Company had a great deal of capital and was busily gearing up for a whiz-bang economy. While at Piper, Rogallo invented a special spoiler for landing controls and a new wing-flap concept. However, he did not actually fly in a hang glider until 1967.

In 1949, Francis Rogallo designed a kite similar to the man-lifters developed at the turn of the century in England. But the Rogallo kite was simple and used an airframe so efficiently that the National Aeronautics and Space Administration (NASA) pumped millions of dollars into man-lifter kite research.

The Rogallo kite was the first unmanned parachute device that could be controlled by remote control. Rogallo's main idea applied the standard hang glider kite configuration to the recovery of missiles and

The Mitchell wing is one of the family of fixed-wing, foot-launched hang gliders. It holds the long-distance record and is usually Number One in its class. The versatility of the Mitchell wing stems from the fact that two people can slip it into a bag and lift the entire wing onto the top of a truck. This class of hang gliders can also be easily motorized.

space modules (even those as large as Saturn third-stage boosters). For reasons still classified, the Rogallo research was suddenly abandoned, but his idea leaked out to more aggressive pioneers, and the modern delta-winged hang glider was born. It is known, however, that NASA has developed a Rogallo vehicle for potential use on Mars.

HANG GLIDER ECONOMICS AND MACHINE-GUN KNOW-HOW

Hang glider designers of the 1970s and 1980s are faced with an almost unbearable dilemma, because the military is always interested in hang gliders. In a shed in Albuquerque, New Mexico, military designers have developed a huge gray fixed-wing hang glider [ostensibly designed for record-breaking long-distance flights], which is little more than a war machine. This prototype is foot-launchable and motorizable, with a fully enclosed cockpit. At the point of takeoff, the pilot jumps inside the bubble, and two doors shut over his or her body.

The complicated controls consist of bicycle hand grips and tractor pedals attached to long cables. These cables control flaps and spoilers inside the wing, which various pilots refer to as Newman's Folly, after its owner-developer, Larry Newman. But the idea may not be as impractical as it seems. Many observers feel that the weight of the craft would crush the pilot on landing, but skid plates, wheels and control parachutes, in tandem with an efficient rotary motor or a light jet, may prevent this, since the lifting capabilities of this fixed-wing, foot-launchable glider are phenomenal. In its prototype format, it can carry a pilot and all necessary gear, instrumentation and fuel (the auxiliary engine can be sealed in a pod overhead), plus light rockets or a scaled-down electronic Gatling gun. There is no doubt that this wing could also be balloon- or tow-launched through clouds and swoop silently down like a falcon for its prey. To prove this point, Newman and two other gents took a balloon ride across the Atlantic with a hang glider attached to the gondola.

Politics influences economics. The president of one hang glider company has stated publicly on numerous occasions that he intends to monopolize the manufacturing of hang gliders worldwide by acquiring all of the smaller companies. It is frightening to think of the consequences, should he succeed. And he may come close—he need only produce a superior product, and this he does; he sells an average of thirty hang gliders per day through worldwide distribution outlets. Only the pilots themselves can thwart these outlandish dreams.

The industry predicts a 25 to 30 percent per annum growth factor until the year 2000. Now, assuming a theoretical company receives a profit of $600 per hang glider, it is no problem to calculate that an aggressively expanding company could easily gross $4 million per year—not bad for a cottage-craft operation which originated in the midst of an inflationary energy crisis!

SELF-POWERED FLIGHT AND THE KREMER AWARD

Money does play a positive role in hang gliding. In 1959 a British industrialist and physical fitness enthusiast decided that human beings could fly under muscle power alone! All the famous aviation prizes had long since been won; military agencies had assumed responsibility for going ever faster through the air, and the only significant aviation threshold still unconquered was human-powered flight (HPF).

Encouraged by friends in the Royal Aeronautical Society, Henry Kremer offered £5,000 sterling for the first successful British effort to attain sustained flight over a figure-eight course laid out between two pylons one-half mile apart, with a 2.5-meter minimum altitude at the beginning and end. Even at this late date, some of the London newspeople scoffed at the idea.

Up to the Kremer Prize epoch, sporadic efforts in HPF, many with the almost idiotic ornithopter or flapping-wing design, some with rubber band assistance for takeoff, and at least one with an inflated wing containing lighter-than-air gas, had been carried out. But many doubted whether actual flight had been achieved and, if so, whether it was exclusively human-powered. The Kremer Prize regulations eliminated all such doubts by carefully screening the various ploys used in getting and/or remaining airborne. Shock-cord launching, lighter-than-air gases, and groundcrew assists were all expressly forbidden in Kremer Prize competition.

While Henry Kremer may have intended to encourage HPF, he was, in effect, defining it. While it may be possible to achieve HPF *without* flying the complete Kremer Prize course, there is broad agreement that any winner of the Kremer Prize has reached and exceeded the elusive goal. In the eight years following the announcement of the prize, several efforts were mounted by qualified British teams, some with very provocative results—"close, but no cigar," as the saying goes. In 1957 the offer was increased to £10,000, and competition was opened to all comers. By 1963, in spite of the doubled inducement, no one had satisfied the difficult demands of the competition, and in 1967 the award was increased to £50,000 (approximately $96,000).

THE GOSSAMER CONDOR

The idea of building a human-powered aircraft with the aid of a computer occurred to Paul MacCready in July, 1976, as he, like Mouillard, was preparing an article comparing the flight of hawks to the flight of hang gliders. He realized that adapting hang glider construction techniques could produce a very light, large, slow-flying vehicle which would be easy to build, modify and repair, and would require little horsepower to keep aloft. MacCready, a full-time aerodynamicist and part-time hang glider and sailplane pilot, had a new spark of interest. Naturally, this spark was fanned by his knowledge of the Kremer Prize.

By September, 1976, the first models to bear the name Gossamer Condor had become realities. The first design had an 88-foot wingspan and weighed 20 kilograms. It was completed in the pavilion where floats for Pasadena's Rose Parade are constructed, but because MacCready and his team had to vacate the pavilion the morning after completion, there was only time for a single test flight. This took place in the Rose Bowl parking lot between midnight and 2 A.M., during a light rain. The tests were successful, but the plane had to be disassembled and hauled to Mohave Airport to be rebuilt.

By November, 1976, the crew had learned some harsh lessons about the behavior of lightweight aircraft, even in light crosswinds, and something about the shortcomings of human power. MacCready began to appreciate why Leonardo da Vinci gave up after eight years, reconciling himself to hang soaring. In one instance, the wing simply collapsed in a minor gust of wind. On the day after Christmas 1976, MacCready's 17-year-old son Parker made an encouraging nonstop flight of 40 seconds. This event buoyed everyone's spirits, and technical development accelerated. At the same time, a serious program of physical and nutritional conditioning for Gossamer Condor pilot candidates continued under the guidance of Joe Mastropaolo of Long Beach State University. Subsequent test flights were made by MacCready's 14-year-old son Tyler. In February, 1977, less wind and more hangar space became a priority, and the entire awkward operation, which now attracted groups of followers, made its way to Shafter Airport near Bakersfield, California.

On August 23, 1977, piloted by a champion bicyclist named Bryan Allen, Paul MacCready's second-stage Gossamer Condor, with a 96-foot wingspan, flew into aviation history by successfully completing the Kremer Prize course at the Shafter Airport. Please recall that this course

The Gossamer Condor breaking the Kremer award record for self-propelled flight.

requires unassisted takeoff and long sustained flight with turns and climbs—a grueling set of tasks for a bicyclist pedaling a propeller-driven vehicle with a complex system of gears and pulleys.

The aircraft took off at 7:30 A.M. and landed 7 minutes 27.5 seconds later. It had taken 6 minutes 22.5 seconds of the flight to complete the official circuit, a figure-eight course around pylons 1/2 mile apart (.80 kilometers), with a 10-foot-high (3-meter) hurdle at the beginning and end, as required by the Kremer Prize rules. The flight speed was between 10 and 11 mph (14 kilometers per hour). The plane traveled 1.35 miles (roughly 2 kilometers) through the air from takeoff to landing.

Even though the final Gossamer Condor, with a wingspan of almost 30 meters, laid justifiable claim to all sorts of aviation superlatives—world's slowest prop-driven airplane, history's lightest wind loading, more flight

(Photo from Howard Siepen)

German flying wing hang glider, 1929, similar to Mitchell wing and other modern small-wing hang gliders. Cockpit was optional.

time than all other human-powered aircraft combined—it was, like the Wright brothers' planes, a shade-tree operation. But, instead of the Wright brothers' two wings, stabilizers and propellers, the Condor had one of each, made from aluminum tubing, balsa wood and corrugated paper and supported by piano wire and nylon cord. The entire plane was covered by transparent Mylar, and a styrofoam sheet held in place with plastic tape gave the cockpit its shape. All of these materials are surprisingly nonexotic, available through any hardware store.

WHAT THE FLIGHT OF THE CONDOR MEANS

By fulfilling the old self-powered prophecy, the Gossamer Condor passed a very significant milestone in aviation history. Ever since engine-powered flight commenced at Kitty Hawk in 1903, the pursuit of

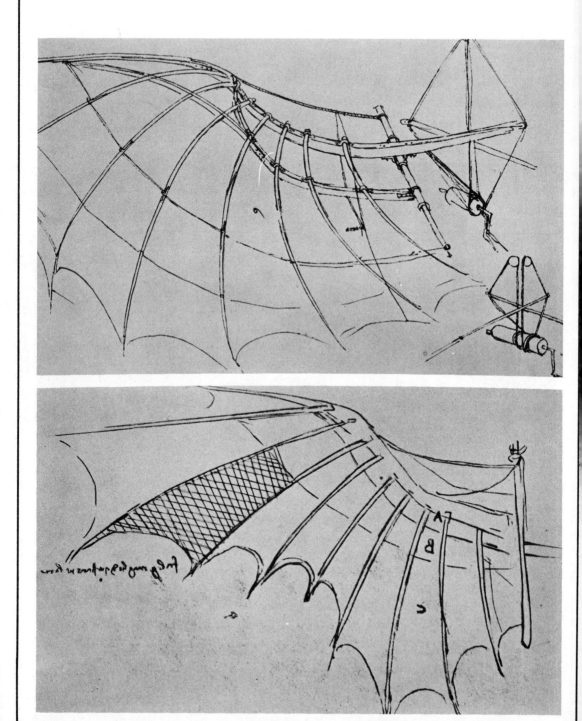

Cross section of da Vinci's Great Swan hang glider.

this goal has been subordinated to the pursuit of more practical (i.e., military) ends. However, for the pioneers, self-powered flight was one of the major goals, and the flight of August 23, 1977, represents its achievement.

Aside from breaking the record, the Condor's future value is clear. As with the Apollo moon mission, the value is not only in the event itself and in raising human eyes to a broader perspective of the universe, but also in the technical spin-offs which arise from every major breakthrough. In the case of MacCready's Condor, the fact that Mylar can be strong enough to support a pilot is certainly intriguing. Of course the questions that must be asked now are: Where will the Condor fly next and who will challenge it?

Most well-informed people realize that the energy crisis is here to stay. The Condor experiments proved that humans could fly on 33 percent of one horsepower. Furthermore, the Gossamer Condor can carry neither bombs nor extra passengers, and its direct descendants will be unwarlike. But there is a growing field of ultralight aircraft that may use Condor designs. There are also many places in the field of energy conservation where flow optimization can pay significant dividends. Anytime a human being moves through a fluid or gas, energy is consumed; conversely, energy is conserved if the task is made easier in some way. Thus, high energy costs provide incentive for conservation in flight. The same ideas may show up in the form of windmills and better streamlining for passenger planes as time goes on.

Paul MacCready reports that for him one of the most valuable spin-offs of the Gossamer Condor program was related to improvements in his own physiology. Under the tutelage of Dr. Joseph Mastropaolo, MacCready and his son Tyler embarked on a rigorous exercise program to put them in condition for the record attempt. In six weeks, MacCready, at age 51, developed the stamina of a good college athlete. His interest in conditioning will be invaluable to him in later years. Mastropaolo, recognizing the need for incentives in physical training, has, for many years, pictured man-powered flight as the ideal motivator.

There were many other payback factors in the success of the Gossamer Condor, but the one which most differentiated it from previous serious human-powered developments was the ease of construction. The vehicle was also easily and inexpensively modified and repaired. A broken wing, although frustrating, meant flights would be delayed only a few days, not a year or a century. This permitted extensive testing (some 400 flights) and systematic evolution of the vehicle through a dozen different versions.

Most other contenders for the Kremer Prize have been more conven-

Jody MacCready

tional looking, but the computer-based plans of the Gossamer Condor made little use of prior concepts. Instead, it evolved from the Kremer Prize flight requirements and nothing else. Simple theory dictated the wingspan, wing area, and flight speed. The computer met the Kremer Prize standards, and the builders simply followed its logical orders.

HOW TO FLY A CONDOR

Like Sinbad's Rok, the Gossamer Condor was a docile behemoth. Its slow speed permitted the pilot to control it easily through takeoffs, turns and landings. In fact, four people who had never before flown any airplane or hang glider flew the Condor with ease. The pilot was seated in a reclining position with both hands free for controls. He could hold the handle of a control cane with one hand and brace himself with the other; raising or lowering the handle tilted the stabilizer to alter its lift. This led the aircraft up or down and also controlled the speed. Rotating the handle left or right moved ailerons on the stabilizer, and a left twist moved the left tip of the stabilizer down, etc. This yawed the plane to the left and also tended to roll it to the left.

For a wide, or open, turn, the pilot used his other hand to twist a lever beside the seat; this caused the tensioner wires to twist the wing. By this means, a left turn moved the left wing tip through the air 60 percent slower than the right wing tip, an action similar to that of a tank or tractor. The wing-twist technique permits a smooth coordinated turn, but it also initiates the turn by a series of bizarre structural interactions which were not overtly predicted by the computer. In a normal airplane, lowering the left aileron and raising the right gives a slight twist which rolls the plane to the right. With the Gossamer Condor, this twist rolls the plane to the left. To paraphrase Robert Burns, The best laid planes of mice and men often go awry. This proves that computers must interact with human software to be effective.

OPTICS FOR HANG GLIDERS

By now it should be obvious that a hang glider is a total system. Its barest form consists of the glider and the biological unit guiding it, i.e., a human being. But other devices, when added to this simple unit, yield unlimited possibilities.

The view through a 20mm wide-angle lens, attached to either a still or a motion picture camera and firmly mounted on the airframe of a hang glider, is nothing short of phenomenal; but the pilot must think the photographs through before launch. Since the camera is fixed, the kite

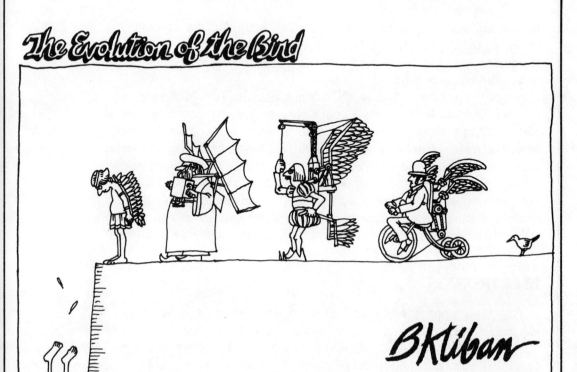

The Evolution of the Bird

BKliban

Copyright 1977 from *Whack Your Porcupine and Other Drawings* by B. Kliban

itself becomes a sort of camera; in this situation, the pilot must know what the lens will reveal without sighting through it. The apertures must be pre-set, for the most part, and the pilot must be able to control the shutter by remote control, cable release or radio actuator. Auto-exposure and auto-focusing devices have opened up even greater possibilities.

In the first phases of hang gliding, the photographers were usually narcissistic: everyone was mugging for home movies and "Look, Ma!" shots. However, as the sport progressed, the seriousness of hang glider camera applications also progressed—with fascinating results! For instance, a hang glider pilot shot the first close-up fly-by of an eagle's nest with normal lenses, and a hang glider pilot shot Teddy Roosevelt's nose on Mt. Rushmore so close that one nostril filled an entire 35mm frame.

Some pilot photographers get carried away. A temporarily brilliant aerobatics pilot from Los Angeles, George Harding, took the first shot of a self-imposed crash. George hooked the remote control release button to the nose of the kite and, at about 10 miles per hour, at night, purposely crashed the kite into a cliff, not only as an existential demonstration of some kind of cosmic disobedience, but to have evidence that hang gliders are safe during controlled crashes. Naturally, the camera was mounted behind the pilot. When interviewed later, George admitted he wanted to see what he would look like while being squashed! Fortunately, he was not hurt.

Not to be outdone, the world champion pilot, Trip Mellinger, took pictures of himself changing a spark plug on his motorized bi-winged glider during a record-breaking flight to Catalina Island from the mainland, and a Hawaiian hang glider pilot took close-up photos of a volcano erupting. He claims the thermals coming out of the volcano were terrific. This obviously attests to the importance of photography as a documentary medium in long-distance flights, if and when photographic proof is needed. Furthermore, inexpensive hang gliders can hover and remain stable over never-before-explored territory, putting costly aerial and scientific views within range of almost anyone.

ELECTRONICS

Two basic applications come to mind when discussing hang glider electronics: CB radio and telemetry. Very few studies have been conducted, but the possibilities of using telemetry—that is, electronic signal-sending devices attached to the pilot and kite (such as analog probes and sensors)—are virtually unlimited. Research could be done on women under flight stress (as opposed to men under the same stress) to ascertain variability in biological functioning and space-readiness profiles. This could be done by training future astronauts and studying their telemetric physiological responses while aloft in a hang glider.

Telemetry can also be used to trace a lost hang glider and to track pilots as they try for distance records such as flying across the English Channel. Needless to say, it could also be used in major world competition to judge pilot performance accurately, just as electronics and computers are used in Grand Prix racing. Telemetry packages are very light and often very powerful. They can be mounted to the glider frame or even built in to reduce drag.

The use of CB radio units on hang gliders is already a reality. Almost every international championship uses a CB walkie-talkie network to put the ground judges in touch with the launch-site personnel, as well as the shuttle truck, when one is used. This says nothing of the usefulness of CB in pilot-to-pilot communications. It is feasible that two pilots could help each other out of a cloud by maintaining CB contact; in any case, it beats shouting against the wind. The English hang gliding school in Bristol uses radio communications in the training of new pilots. These pilots learn faster and have fewer crashes.

The long-distance barograph and certain soaring variometers also deserve mention. The barograph is a sealed device that is used on long-distance and altitude record-breaking attempts. This device keeps a printed record of altitude. It was adapted to hang gliders from sailplanes and is essentially the same device, with lighter components designed to scale. The barograph must be sealed by a hang gliding official and must be opened only in front of an official, or the record is considered invalid. It must be accurate, reliable and impervious to weather conditions, since a delicate paper graph is contained inside the glass case.

The electronic soaring variometer (discussed briefly in Chapter 3) lets out a loud screech as the glider ascends and a low tone as the glider descends; thus, the speed and intensity of the tone can guide the pilot in low-visibility conditions, such as may be encountered in a cloud. The standard variometer is not much help in blind flying, as it reads out as a needle indicator. Naturally, bright light-emitting devices (LEDs) will take over in this field, as the LED digital readout can be seen clearly in the dark.

The future of hang gliding obviously holds many challenges, riddles and secrets; but most of these will be solved with the application of motors and electronic devices. In fact, laser systems, electronic control servos, solar battery applications and all sorts of other exotics are already on the drawing boards.

THE BALLOON LAUNCH

The history of hang gliding closely parallels the development of the hot air balloon, and now that both sports have emerged as advanced forms in the new age of technology, it seems only natural that hang gliders should be launched from balloons.

English hang glider pilots have long dreamed of crossing the English Channel without the aid of motorization, but to do this balloons were necessary. In 1977 three pilots—two men and a woman—flew from Dover to Calais with the aid of a balloon launch—a launch not uncommon either in Europe or America. The gliders and pilots were attached to the hot air balloon by ring release cables, and as the balloon ascended, so did the gliders. At a prearranged height the glider pilots triggered the release cables, which remained attached to the balloon. From an altitude of more than 1,000 meters, the balloon-launched gliders were able to catch thermals and vespers which took them across the Channel.

Not to be outdone, one American company simultaneously drop-tested nine piloted gliders from a balloon with special rigging designed for that purpose—and although the flight was uneventful, it did prove that the

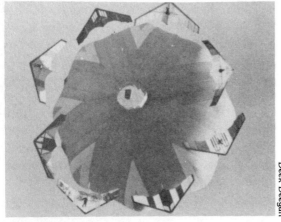

Deek Deegan

Multiple balloon launch, Escape Country, California.

wedding of balloon and hang glider is possible. Subsequent unpiloted launches have been made from balloons to test new wing configurations and new parachute designs.

MOTORIZED HANG GLIDERS: THE CONTROVERSY

Those who fail to learn from history are doomed to relive it. Hang gliding was originally a pure form of gliding research. When the Wrights and others motorized the glider, the airplane became an inevitable political instrument—each designer, each country flexing muscles and rattling sabres at Mach Four.

Modern hang gliding faces the same schism, this time as a repeat performance. There seem to be two schools—the pure flight Ecogliders and the Hot Rodders—with many pilots, either unable or unwilling to decide, planting a foot squarely in each camp. Of course there are moder-

Motorized bi-wings waiting for the wind.

Harrison

ates who wish to use the motor as an auxiliary, but there is a growing awareness that motorization will bring the fast buck to the barnstorming acrobatic stunt pilot or the hell-bent marathon pilot who sees cross-country racing as the pot of gold at the end of the thermal.

Motorized hang gliders are in their infancy. While some designers are talking about fully enclosed wings, such as the Canard and the Mitchell wing, and the use of triple-weird engines, such as compressed-air bottles for Jet Assisted Takeoff (JATOs), most motor jockeys are stuck with trying to adapt a chain-saw motor with a mouth-held clothespin throttle, or coax more revolutions from a mixture of benzine and airplane gas, because the octane ratings of automobile gasoline are unreliable. In short, a huge gap exists between the elite technologists at the top of the hang glider design ladder, most of whom started at the middle and worked up, and the poor Sunday-afternoon sky-out who has to grind five days a week to finance that glorious Sunday in the updrafts. It is unfortunate, but this social schism may prove to be the undoing of hang gliding as a sport, unless, of course, the pilots themselves develop a flexible non-hierarchical top-level organization which consists of nothing but pilots.

INTERNATIONAL HANG GLIDING: THE GRAND TOUR

International hang gliding possibilities are almost unlimited when all of the cliffs and hills in the world are considered. The following is a list of a few of the more public and spectacular locales in the order rated by a concensus of European and American pilots.

Kossen, Austria

Kossen, located in the Austrian Alps, is one of the most incredible soaring sites in the world. Ski lifts transport the pilots to many different launch points; grassy meadows serve as landing areas; thermals abound, and where there are no thermals, ridge lift seems to be available.

Dover, England

The beautiful white cliffs of Dover are ridge-lift naturals, and by skillful maneuvering, pilots can land back on the ridge. Winds from the Channel are often mild breezes, creating smooth updrafts at the cliffs. A number of balloon-launched flights have been made from Dover, and a few of these have ended happily in France. Hang gliding the English Channel is all the rage at Dover.

Glacier Point, Yosemite, California

The exotic granite mounds of Yosemite National Park are perfect backdrops for Hang IV takeoffs; but the crosswinds are treacherous, and a number of accidents have ended in casualties. Out of concern, the park authorities have forbidden all hang gliding in the park, and have attempted to ban hang gliding in all federal reserves across the nation. This ban would be impossible to enforce, since the air above the park is not the park; but sneaking a hang glider past the ranger station is a trick in itself.

Torrey Pines, La Jolla, California

Torrey Pines, near San Diego, is the classic location for Pacific ridge soaring. In fact, Torrey is so often soarable that the advanced pilots call it Borey Torrey, implying that Torrey is a perfect place for Hang II and Hang III pilots.

Fort Funstan, San Francisco, California

Fort Funstan is an old World War II gun emplacement, situated on dunes and ending at the Pacific Ocean in a sheer sand cliff covered with ice grass. The winds at Funstan are tricky, but many pilots cut their teeth at Funstan, and it will always be an exciting place!

Cerro Gordo, California

Cerro Gordo means fat cloud. It is from here that most of the world's long-distance soaring records have been established. In 1977 a pilot named George Worthington took off from Cerro Gordo and wound up 110 miles away at a brothel near Beatty, Nevada. He had traveled across the center of the Mojave Desert at about 10,000 feet, with excellent tailwinds providing propulsion, all the while using "cumes" and thermals to gain altitude. Needless to say, the working girls were delighted to greet their unique visitor from the sky. They also witnessed the record and signed the official U.S.H.G.A. record form.

Sylmar, California

The north end of the San Fernando Valley offers a smog-free mountain called Sylmar Peak, which is soarable at least 75 percent of the time from many directions, because, like the Swiss Alps, it offers both thermals and ridge lift simultaneously. Unfortunately, the town of Sylmar is only marginally cooperative, and the pilots must avoid high-voltage wires in order to land.

The Hawaiian Islands

The many cliffs in Hawaii at Oahu, Maui and Wiamea Bay are ideal for duration records, as the wind almost never dies and ridge lift is constant and smooth. Not only is the jungle vegetation beautiful, but it has cushioned more than one crash. Hang gliding in Hawaii is a natural development of ocean surfing, and many glider pilots are also proficient in a tube at the Banzai pipeline.

Grouse Mountain, British Columbia

Like Sylmar Peak, Grouse Mountain is close to town; in fact, the municipal transportation system of North Vancouver operates a shuttle bus to the Grouse Mountain sky car. Grouse is a fine example of year-round location, as skiing takes precedence in the winter months. The mountain can be seen from Howe Sound and from Lions Gate Bridge in Vancouver, and championship hang gliding winds are excellent in the summer and fall.

Lookout Mountain, Chattanooga, Tennessee

Chattanooga is turned on to hang gliding, and it has become Chattanooga's most prestigious local activity. Hang gliders can be seen mounted on cars everywhere. The area abounds in all classes of hang gliding takeoff points. Consequently, the world's first hang gliding hotel and resort was founded in Chattanooga. This resort features a pro shop, a pool, a sauna, and a bunkhouse for under-capitalized bachelor pilots.

Australia

As with Hawaii, very little can be said about the Land Down Under except that Australian hang gliding was developed to a high art by an Australian named Bill Bennett, who made the sport popular in North America. There are so many ridges and cliffs along the Australian and New Zealand coasts that listing them would be impossible. Furthermore, these sites are jealously guarded by the local pilots who are, like anyone else, territorial beasts, especially when the sky is up and optimal.

Bill Bennett over the Statue of Liberty, July 4, 1969.

Heavener, Oklahoma

Heavener is located approximately 60 miles south of Fort Smith, Arkansas, in the Ozarks. The weather at Heavener is not good for hang gliding all year round, but in the spring Bear Mountain can be breathtaking for Hang IV-rated pilots. The launch site is at least 1,000 feet above the landing area, and a green valley, which incidentally is peppered with moonshine stills, stretches out for hundreds of miles in all directions.

Grandfather Mountain, North Carolina

Grandfather Mountain, situated in the Smokies near Linville, is a veritable pilot's dream. Launchings can be made in almost any direction, weather is ideal much of the year, and thermals are plentiful. A number of masters' competitions have been held at Grandfather, and the local people react very favorably to the colorful kites and pilots.

Grandfather Mountain launch point, North Carolina. One of the best flight locations in North America.

Bettina Gray

Telluride, Colorado. The Rockies provide year-round ridge lifts.

Bettina Gray

Telluride, Colorado

No place in the world can equal Telluride for rapid lift from takeoff. The world's foot-launch altitude records are broken here without the need of balloons. Telluride is located in the midst of the Colorado Rockies. These mountains are the Himalayas of North America, and Telluride is one of the Rockies' finest ski resorts. Hang glider pilots have been known to fly all the way down to the village of Telluride and land in a parking lot to catch a beer before returning to the top.

Mt. Cranmore, North Conway, New Hampshire

Mt. Cranmore, in the heart of New Hampshire, provides excellent snow skiing in the winter and top-flight hang gliding in the dry months. A number of national and international meets have been held there, and the local accommodations are far above average. The New Hampshire trees are a picture not to be missed as they change colors in the fall, because from 3,000 feet, the colors seem to melt into brown and yellow puddles interrupted by jagged rock structures.

Cape Cod: Tonset Dunes, Chatham Light, Wellfleet Audubon Sanctuary

A number of cliffs along the Cape form perfect takeoff points for hang gliding. Tonset Dunes has the peculiar distinction of being the only place in the world where the full moon casts a shadow as it seems to rise from the sea exactly at sunset. The best soaring winds occur in the winter, when the snow mixes with the sand. The winds off the Atlantic are icy, but they are smooth. Hot cranberry wine after the flight makes it all worthwhile. New Englanders know that a winter on the Cape is called "The Seee Shoor Cuoor," and now hang gliding has become an added attraction. Strangely enough, the first hang gliding school in America was started at South Wellfleet in the 1930s by German pilots.

The list could go on *ad infinitum.* The Danish Hang Gliding Club has found a cliff site near Copenhagen which they claim is excellent; in Holland, between Zandvoort and Wassenaar, pilots find high sand cliffs that are graced with both windmills and oil wells. At Wiltshire in the south of England, a natural glacial moraine and a series of old mounds and monadnocks have created a wind bowl which provides excellent soaring. Lift-off can be accomplished from many points around the rim of the

Soaring Cape Cod.

bowl, depending upon the direction of the prevailing winds. The only limitation at the wind bowl is the fact that hang gliders tend to disturb neighboring chicken coops; it seems the chickens take the gliders for hawks and refuse to lay, thus disrupting the Wiltshire economy.

There are hundreds of jealously guarded sites all over the world, and to Hang IV-rated pilots, these are the succulent morsels that can never be mentioned in print.

THE SPORT

In spite of all arguments, many will consider hang gliding a dangerous activity restricted to the insane. The grandchildren of the scoffers who laughed at the Wright brothers are now convinced that the moon landings never happened, and all attempts at their conversion will end in abject failure. Those who do have an interest in hang gliding as a competitive sport will need to know a bit more about the future of the sport and the subdivisions of competition. Hang gliding can be divided roughly into five areas of competitive specialization, although top pilots must be proficient in all areas. These areas are Cross-Country, Aerobatics, Course Competition, Altitude Soaring and Duration Soaring.

Cross-Country or Long-Distance Soaring (Pure or Motorized)

Cross-country competition emphasizes miles or kilometers. Time is of secondary importance, although time/distance ratio is definitely a sign of true skill. Five hundred miles or 800 kilometers in one day with no motor is not unthinkable if the right glider and the right pilot meet the ideal weather conditions. Most records are broken in June and July in North America, but the English Channel has been flown in the late autumn on numerous occasions.

Aerobatics

Aerobatic hang gliding emphasizes use of aerial ballet and body action to create stunt forms and maneuvers like 720° turns and wing-overs. It is probably best described as a form of airborne *tai-chi* (an Oriental meditation exercise) which places emphasis on give and take, pressure and release of pressure, Yin and Yang. Aerobatic flying is a spectacular event, but it is generally not included in international competition.

Course Competition (Solo, One-on-One or Multiple)

Course competition is a competitive format often favored by pilots in hang gliding meets. The pilot must complete a designated course and perform a number of maneuvers, such as a 360° turn. He or she may take optional pylons in the course and land on target for extra points. Each course is different, dependent on location and air conditions.

Altitude Soaring

Altitude gain is an esoteric aspect of hang gliding competition that uses speed of ascent and final altitude as competitive variables. Altitudes of 10,000 feet are not uncommon, but the danger of hypoxia, or oxygen starvation, is very real at greater altitudes.

Mirror marking device for course competition.

Bettina Gray

Duration Soaring

It is inevitable that someone will officially soar from dawn to dawn some day; this may have already happened unofficially. The idea in marathon soaring is to stay aloft as long as possible. No one really knows the limits of human ability in this area of wind sailing, but research is constant, and long flights are commonplace in Hawaii.

THE HANG V RATING

Soaring was the goal of the original non-motorized aviators. They saw the possibilities in human-powered flight or in extended glider flight, but the motor temporarily won the day. If only those early pioneers could see the art as it now exists, perhaps they would have been spared some pain. The modern hang glider pilot is capable of things no pioneer could have imagined except in a wild imagining. A brief look at the qualifications for a Hang V rating will demonstrate the extent of progress.

The Hang V rating is really an honorary degree, and very few pilots have achieved this status. A Hang V rating is only obtainable after the pilot has maintained a Hang IV rating for at least one year. The Hang V rating represents a master license, but it is also like the Academy Awards' Oscar—largely influenced by the personal popularity of the pilot-candidate. A Hang V pilot must demonstrate skill in the following areas:

Dealing with Turbulence

A Hang V pilot must be able to demonstrate controlled flight under various conditions and multiple variations in wind directions and velocity. These require smooth but quick control and adjustments in normally dangerous conditions.

Altitude Flight

A Hang V pilot must also be able to fly above 1,000 feet for more than 10 minutes. At this altitude, the pilot must be able to perform 360° turns in both directions.

Cliff Soaring and Thermals

Any Hang V-rated pilot must be able to control all variables at a cliff site at least 200 feet (60 meters) high. The launches must be unassisted in strong lift conditions; safe landings must also be demonstrated here. Thermals must be found and used correctly for proficiency at this level.

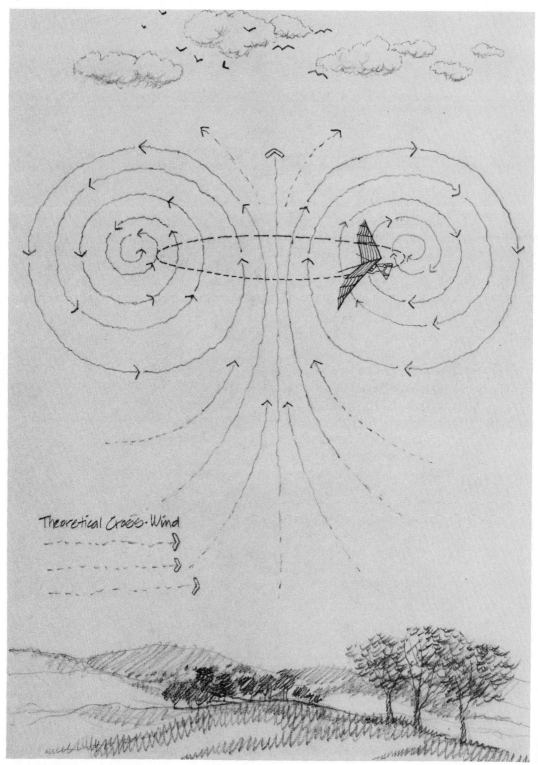

Theoretical Cross-Wind

Thermaling is a necessary skill for advanced hang gliding ratings.

Open ridge lift and rotor utilization.

Cross-Country

A Hang V pilot must be able to fly cross-country. To do this, the pilot must be able to negotiate canyon conditions and dives and be skilled in wind control and thermal lift control. All Hang V-rated pilots must be able to determine wind direction while in flight from observation of natural phenomena (e.g., observation of tree branches, whitecaps on waves). They must be able to recognize landing areas and demonstrate flat 360° turns with little or no banking. All of these must be accomplished in multiple wind conditions.

THE WORLD CUP INTERNATIONAL COMPETITION

Competitive hang gliding is a non-sexist sport. No handicaps or ratings are based solely on the sex of the pilot. Women compete equally with men in all classes, because sheer physical strength is not a factor, although stamina is important. In fact, women often beat men in across-the-board hang gliding competition. The determining factors are the wing loading and the performance characteristics of the glider itself. In hang gliding, the wind does the balancing, not the pilots or the armchair handicappers.

From close observation, there seem to be three distinct forms of international hang gliding competition based on the three basic hang glider configurations. In a strange way, the personalities of the pilots correlate with the type of glider they choose. First comes the pilot who flies Class One and is dependent on a basic or slightly modified Rogallo configuration. This is a deltoid-shaped kite, often limited in maneuverability. It is an excellent kite, safe for both beginners and advanced pilots.

The second type of pilot prefers a kite based on the bat wing. This kite represents an advance over the Rogallo design at the expense of a small loss in stability. The batwing gliders are easily identified by two distinct characteristics: first, the wing tips are truncated like those of a folded paper airplane, and second, batten sticks strengthen the wing and stop the dacron material from lufting in turns, especially during acrobatic wing-overs and loops. The batwing flyer tends to be interested in a more gymnastic form of the sport.

The third type of flyer is interested in fixed-wing gliders. These easily motorized gliders are ideal for long-distance cross-country soaring. They can be lightweight solid wings made from dacron stretched over frames, or they can be bi-winged configurations.

Advanced international competition in hang gliding has come about only because the airframe structure of the hang gliders and the physical fitness of the pilots have far exceeded the level of the early pioneers. The standard ripless dacron sailcloth, which can withstand incredible stresses, has only been available to the public since the 1950s. Aluminum tubing and the design techniques used in hang gliding are ancient ideas that have finally been perfected. The physical fitness and training of pilots have also been greatly improved. All of these factors combined have made hang gliding a competitive sport, more exciting and demanding than skiing, tennis or Grand Prix racing.

In one decade, hang gliding as a sport has grown rapidly. International hang gliding associations and the manufacturers together have developed its safety and prestige; hang gliding competition has reached the status of auto racing or world class skiing. Of course, any cigar-box mechanic can staple some plastic sheets to a bamboo frame and jump off a cliff, but the top-level hang glider pilot must meet rigorous standards.

The types of competition are varied: some courses are laid out in an S-turn; some are triangular; some have high cliff launch points; others launch from hillsides; some courses require two or more pilots to compete in the air one-to-one, as in surfing contests; some require individual efforts that test form and efficiency in various categories, such as thermaling, 360° turns, banking, lift stability duration, distance and target landing.

In most cases, qualification heats and regional screening competitions enable the best and most dedicated pilots to move forward—quickly.

POLITICS

Under no circumstances can it be said that hang gliding is a North American sport. True, hang gliding has been greatly developed in North America, but Japanese, Australian and European competitions have been held successfully for many years. In fact, Bill Bennett, who is considered by some to be the granddaddy of the sport, is an Australian. (He was arrested for circumnavigating the Statue of Liberty in the 1960s.) Hang gliding is anything but secular and parochial; it is an open, non-discriminating sport. International teams do take on a team pride, but this is a healthy and necessary aspect of any international competition.

Most experts predict that hang gliding will be an Olympic sport before the year 2000. This possibility raises the obvious political problem of who gets paid and who gets subsidized, who flies at his or her own expense and who flies at the manufacturers' expense? Further complications arise from conflict between naïve hang gliding regulatory bodies which run on the love of the art and certain aggressive sports conglomerates. One of these, a Texas-based football franchise, seeks to achieve control of all sports media within the next fifty years, thus robbing hang gliding of most of its charm. If these cartels do succeed in dominating hang gliding, then the best pilots will be forced to exchange serenity and art for a handful of silver; they themselves will eventually be bought and traded like football players, and their long-sought freedom will be short-lived.

Even now, most top-level pilots agree that hang gliding should remain an amateur or semi-pro sport. This stance protects the pilot who wishes to soar just for the intrinsic relaxation of hang gliding. The promoters forget that hang gliding can and should be a meditative event of the most important kind—a technique for turning inward and meditating on survival.

Because hang gliding is the only activity yet discovered that affords almost anyone the ability to fly at pocketbook prices, modern hang glider pilots are often referred to as impoverished astronauts. But there is no such thing as an ex-hang glider pilot. In this sport, now is reality. The more flying hours logged, the more the concept of now-ness, and what is referred to in Zen as is-ness, takes hold.

THE UNBELIEVABLE FUTURE OF THE HANG GLIDER

Hang gliding is again starting to divide into the two schools mentioned by Charles H. Gibbs-Smith in *The Invention of the Airplane, 1799–1909.*

Gibbs stated that at the onset of motorized flight, two distinct pilot and design groups emerged. The first group he called chauffeurs, because they saw the airplane as a flying automobile possessed of brute force, and as an extension of a penis. Gibbs called the second group aeronauts, because they dreamed of self-propelled flight. They avoided the noisy and dirty motor altogether and concentrated on developing the foot-launched glider. Although the chauffeurs won the first round, modern hang gliding is really the province of the aeronauts. Motorization is creeping into hang gliding, but the motorless wing will always be the *sine qua non* of the sport.

In the future, hang gliding will be an everyday affair. Hang gliders will be both more and less expensive than they are now, and will soar higher, go faster, and stay longer. A fully enclosed glider, like Larry Newman's wing, the Mitchell wing and a strange ship called *The Canard,* will be able to perform all of these feats and many more—the future of hang gliding is truly unlimited.

HANG GLIDING AND THE NEW ALCHEMY

Hang gliding is a phenomenon of the suburbs—for some reason urban-centered people don't take to the air—yet hang gliding is no more a fad than flight itself, and the quest for flight seems to have been a common quest for thousands of years. Anyone who thinks hang gliding is a temporary sport is simply unaware of the factors that motivate fads and fancies. Clearly, the sport of hang gliding has already grown beyond the vision of the fickle public—a credulous news media ready to pounce on the slightest hint of bad news, and the frightened parents of adventuresome teenagers. Hang gliding is a safe sport, and the equipment is growing in safety factors each year.

In a way, hang gliding is diagnostic; it tends to separate the silly from the sublime. To test this statement drive to a well-known hang gliding spot and make some observations. Note that the very best flyers are doing most of the flying and they tend to control who flies—social pressure can do wonders to regulate safety rules, and that is what has happened in hang gliding.

Harrison

St. Michael, from the chapel, Mount St. Michael, Brittany, France.

In the final analysis hang gliding has afforded human beings another opportunity for personal development similar to the kind of psychotherapeutic reprogramming that has recently been achieved through the study of dolphin behavior. In an indirect way, hang gliding is a data-collecting operation for the study of the wisdom of birds —the osprey, owl, hummingbird and gull. Foot-launched flight is still another channel for human evolution.

Most hang glider pilots seem to believe that once individuals have flown they will always quest for flight because they will realize that they have flown before—in their dreams. Subconsciously, everyone is touched by hang gliding as it pushes evolution a slight notch forward. The world is changing, change is eternal, and hang gliding is simply one more method of change. More than any other technique of individual development, including LSD and all forms of psychotherapy, hang gliding separates the chaff from the wheat, the valued from the unusable; it defines the future and restates again and again the emerging realization that technology is magic.

> . . . and they had the hands of a man
> under their wings
> on their four sides;
> and they four had their faces
>   and their wings.
>   [Ezekiel 1:8]

(Courtesy of The Garden of Monsters, Villa Borghese, Bomarzo.)

The words carved around the lips of the monster read: Ogni Pensiero Vola, *"Great Thoughts Take Flight."*

Glossary of Hang Gliding Terms

The study of hang gliding as a sport and especially as a form of technology is growing every day. This glossary is designed to provide basic information; but slang terms must also be learned, and these, of course, change with the times.

Angle of attack—The angle between the glider wing and the wind it flies into.

Anvil cloud—The spreadout, cirriform, ice-crystal top of a cumulonimbus cloud which, after it has blown downwind from the generating mass, often looks like the overhanging end of an anvil.

Aspect ratio—The ratio between the wingspan of a hang glider and the average width of its wing (see *Chord*).

Attitude—The position of a hang glider in relation to the horizontal. Straight and level flight is considered normal.

Bank—The sideways tip or roll of a hang glider while making turns.

Barograph—A recording barometer, calibrated in altitude instead of pressure. Sealed soaring barographs verify altitude, altitude gained, and the fact that a hang glider was continuously aloft on any given flight.

Buffeting (lufting)—The drumming sound made by a wing as it approaches a stall.

Check point—A landmark easily recognized on the ground, used for navigation and checking the progress of a flight.

Chord—The width of a wing; *mean chord* is the *average* width of a wing.

Cirrus—High, transparent, ice-crystal cloud, usually 30,000 to 40,000 feet (10,000 meters) above the surface of the earth.

Cloudbase—The flattish bottom of a cumulus cloud which marks the condensation point of rising warm air converting to vapor.

Cloud street—A series of aligned cumulus clouds under which a hang glider can be flown straight, often at high speed, without the necessity of circling to maintain altitude.

Convection—Vertical movement in the air caused by thermal activity.

Crabbing—When flying crosswind, a pilot counteracts drift by crabbing, or nosing into the wind enough to maintain a desired track over the ground.

Crosswinds—Winds moving across the direction of flight, causing linear sideways motion; correction for this wind is sometimes called trim.

Cumulonimbus—A towering cumulus cloud which has developed into a rain cloud; it often produces lightning, thunder, hail, and other theatrical effects. Some violent clouds of this type, called thunderheads, make tornadoes.

Cumulus—Any of a series of clouds having vertical development, as opposed to the horizontal development of sheet clouds, which stretch out in thin layers.

Dead or stable air—Air without convective vertical motion; green air.

Drag—All factors acting against lift and thrust, namely friction against the hull and the wing edge.

Dust devil—A thermal whirlwind that picks up dust and debris.

Flying speed—Minimum airspeed necessary for the wings to support flight.

G force (gravity force)—A human being standing on the ground is exposed to 1 G, one gravity force. If that person weighs 200 pounds and steps on a scale, it will indicate 200 pounds. When a hang glider is making a turn or pulling out of a dive, the pilot's effective weight is increased by centrifugal force. If the effective weight is 600 pounds, the pilot is being exposed to 3 Gs, or three times gravity. (This extreme analogy is only an illustration.)

Garbage—Items attached to a hang glider that provide drag, such as landing gear, struts, flying wires, radio antennae, temperature gauges, instruments, etc.

Glide angle—The angle at which a hang glider approaches the earth under various conditions of flight, or the angle of glide necessary to reach a specific destination. If a hang glider has a maximum glide angle of six to one, then starting from a height of one mile above the earth, it can land six miles away in any direction, assuming level terrain, dead air, and no wind.

Glide ratio—A measurement that relates the downward distance any given wing can attain in calm air to the starting height. Hang gliders tend to drop in a smooth line, and must use thermals and updrafts to rise. Only motorized craft can rise under all conditions.

Gravity—Static downward pull, usually a constant factor expressed as G force when resisted.

Gross load—The total weight of a hang glider ready to fly, including that of the pilot, his equipment and his baggage.

Gust load—Structural loads imposed by air turbulence.

Hypoxia—Oxygen starvation.

Level flight—Traditionally, level flight is achieved when all factors acting on the plane (in this case, the hang glider) are equal; this means that lift, drag, thrust and gravity must all cancel out as forces.

Lift—All forces acting on the wing that cause it to gain altitude. In conventional airplanes, the thrust of the plane causes the wind to be swept over the wing. The amount of lift is determined by the shape and length of the wing, coupled with many other subtle factors.

Lift-to-drag ratio (L/D)—A somewhat complex mathematical formula that defines and determines the glide ratio.

Load—All forces acting upon a hang glider structure in flight. Total load is sometimes considered in its component parts (*see* Gross load; Gust load; Maneuvering load; Static load; Useful load).

Maneuvering load—Loads imposed by use of controls in flight maneuvers.

Micrometeorology—The technical knowledge of meteorology and weather conditions that must be learned by all pilots and sailors. These are the factors in local weather conditions that are too small to be of interest to major weather-reporting agencies. The pilot must develop a hyper-awareness of the immediate environment.

Overdeveloped sky—Cumulonimbus activity that has reached a state where it will hinder soaring flight through production of rainstorms, hail or false cirrus blowoff, which cuts down or stops thermal generation.

Penetration—Capacity for making forward progress through the air at little expense of altitude.

Ridge lift—Up-air coming off a ridge; to maintain flight by using the upcurrent on the windward side of a ridge, cliff or mountain.

Rotor—The area of violent turbulence under a mountain wave, often marked by a ragged cumulus cloud, known either as a rotor-cloud or a roll-cloud; also, the top wind above a ridge.

Sink—Downward motion of the air.

Skid—Sideways motion toward the outside of a turn caused by insufficient bank.

Slip—Sideways motion toward the inside of a turn caused by too steep a bank or not enough rudder.

Soar—To fly a heavier-than-air craft without engine power, flight being sustained by upcurrents in the air; to gain altitude.

Span—The dimension of a hang glider measured from wing tip to wing tip.

Speed to fly—The speed that will give maximum cross-country speed in any situation. It is dependent upon past thermal strength, anticipated thermal strength, and encountered sink. Speed-to-fly rings are normally attached to the variometers of contest hang gliders. The original cross-country speed-to-fly technique was worked out by Dr. Paul MacCready, Jr.

Spiral—Circling flight with either a gain or loss of altitude.

Spiral dive (death dive)—A phenomenon occurring accidentally in blind flight, in which the hang glider begins a turn, the nose gradually drops and speed builds up. The pilot reduces speed, but only succeeds in tightening the turn. If the situation is not corrected, the wings generally collapse.

Stall—A condition in which airflow over the wing becomes turbulent and disturbed so that the wing loses lift, causing the hang glider to fall. Usually caused by lack of flying speed.

Static load—Weight of the empty glider.

Terminal velocity—The highest speed possible in a prolonged vertical dive. In a modern hang glider, structural failure would occur only in approaching or recovering from a terminal velocity dive.

Thermal—A bubble or comparatively small mass of rising heated air. A few thermals are too small to keep a hang glider aloft; others contain more than a cubic mile of air.

Thermal soar—To soar, usually by circling, in rising bubbles or masses of heated air. Thermal soaring requires atmospheric instability but is independent of wind and terrain. Most present-day soaring is done in thermals.

Thermal strength—The speed at which air in a thermal is rising. Depending on velocity, thermals are called strong or weak. Thermal strength is generally expressed in meters per second, or hundreds of feet per minute.

Thrust—The forward motion of the wing, regardless of its propulsion system. Glider thrust is wind-propelled, but jets also provide thrust.

Tip vortex—The whirling of air around the wing tip of a bird or hang glider in flight, caused by the fact that there is high pressure underneath the wing and lower pressure above. Tip vortices behind large jet aircraft can cause fatal damage to light aircraft flying into them too soon after the passage.

Triggering temperature—The temperature to which air must rise in order to start thermals on a soaring day.

Triggering time—The time at which triggering temperature is reached.

Useful load—Maximum allowable weight of the pilot and all equipment.

Variometer—A highly sensitive rate-of-climb instrument which approaches instantaneous reaction speed. Modern variometers are often equipped with audio units which report the rate of climb or descent by the pitch of their whine. Advanced pilots react automatically to the stimulus, freeing their eyes for a study of soaring conditions in the sky.

Vertigo—Dizziness, panic and nausea caused by spatial disorientation in flight. Sometimes vertigo is caused by the misinterpretation of visual signals to the brain.

Wing loading—Total weight of an aircraft divided by the number of square feet of wing area, expressed in pounds per square foot.

Zero sink—When the upward motion in the air exactly equals the minimum sinking rate of a soaring hang glider. When flying at zero sink, there is neither gain nor loss of altitude.

Index

RICKS COLLEGE
DAVID O. McKAY LRC
REXBURG, IDAHO 83440

WITHDRAWN

DAVID O. McKAY LIBRARY
BYU-IDAHO